ORIGAMI
HOLIDAYS

Duy Nguyen

Sterling Publishing Co., Inc.
New York

Design by Judy Morgan
Edited by Claire Bazinet

Library of Congress Cataloging-in-Publication Data

Nguyen, Duy, 1960-
    Origami holidays / Duy Nguyen.
        p. cm.
    Includes index.
    ISBN 0-8069-7887-2
    1. Origami. 2. Holiday decorations. I. Title.

    TT870 .N487 2002
    736'.982--dc21

                         2002021695

10 9 8 7 6 5 4 3 2 1

Published by Sterling Publishing Company, Inc.
387 Park Avenue South, New York, N.Y. 10016
© 2002 by Duy Nguyen
Distributed in Canada by Sterling Publishing
℅ Canadian Manda Group, One Atlantic Avenue, Suite 105
Toronto, Ontario, Canada M6K 3E7
Distributed in Great Britain and Europe by Chris Lloyd at Orca Book
Services, Stanley House, Fleets Lane, Poole BH15 3AJ, England
Distributed in Australia by Capricorn Link (Australia) Pty. Ltd.
P.O. Box 704, Windsor, NSW 2756 Australia
Printed in China

Sterling ISBN 0-8069-7887-2

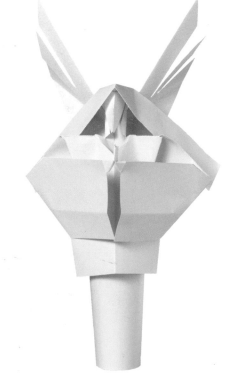

Contents

Foreword 4
Introduction 4
Basic Instructions 5
Symbols & Lines 5

Basic Folds 6
    kite fold ◆ valley fold ◆ mountain fold
    inside reverse fold ◆ outside reverse fold
    pleat fold ◆ pleat fold reverse
    squash fold I ◆ squash fold II
    inside crimp fold ◆ outside crimp fold

Base Folds 10
    base fold I ◆ base fold II ◆ base fold III

Origami Projects

Jack o' Lantern	14	Snowman	54
Scarecrow	18	Kris Kringle	58
Cat's Skull	26	Santa Claus	68
Grim Reaper	30	Reindeer	78
Witch	38	Santa's Sleigh	82
Gremlin Mask	44	Easter Bunny	86
Angel	48	Easter Basket	92

Index 96

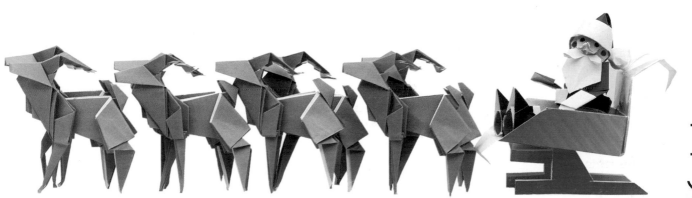

Foreword

Traditionally, a person practicing the "art" of origami works only with one or two square sheets of paper, without any cutting and pasting—or, at least, severely limiting it. The idea is to express one's creativity *wholly* through the art of folding paper—and folding paper exclusively. This means, however, that many finished origami projects have a two-dimensional look and they may even be unrecognizable, due to the simplicity of the traditional form. Many of these origami figures, of course, don't need much folding, or cutting or pasting, to have a beautiful finished look. They are not, however, three-dimensional.

Introduction

When I first began learning origami, I struggled with even the simplest folds, such as the valley, mountain, and pleat folds. When trying to fold an object, I had to look back at the opening chapter again and again to review these basic folds and how to do them. I would also look ahead, at the diagram showing the next step of whatever project I was folding, to see how it *should* look, to be sure that I was following the instructions correctly. Looking ahead at the "next step," the result of a fold, is a very good way for a beginner to learn origami.

Another way to make learning origami easier is to create "construction lines" before doing a complex fold. By this I mean to pre-fold, then unfold, to crease the form and create guidelines. For example: when getting ready to fold a pleat fold reverse or

In this book, I have focused on the creation of three-dimensional objects, using the untraditional origami techniques of cutting and gluing as needed and also multiple sheets of various sizes. The objective was to eliminate, for these holiday decorations, folds that can distort the look of the finished origami while, at the same time, make it easier to shape and recreate them. This book, therefore, combines complex origami folds with the simple cut-and-paste activities that allow children to first express their budding creativity. The result is, I hope, an introduction to the origami art, as well as a fun book of holiday papercraft.

inside and outside reverse folds, if you pre-crease, by using mountain and valley folds, the finished fold is more likely to match the one shown in the book. When your finished folds look different, due to fold lines being at slightly different angles, it can cause confusion and throw you off. It is also important to make good clean fold lines. Well-made construction lines are helpful when you want to unfold the form slightly in order to make another fold easier.

By using these learning techniques, you should have no problem catching on to the basics of origami and performing folds with fewer mistakes. The step-by-step instructions and clearly marked folds given here will quickly have you handcrafting a houseful of fun-to-do holiday decorations.

Duy Nguyen

Basic Instructions

Paper: The best paper to use for traditional origami is very thin, keeps a crease well, and folds flat. You can use plain white paper (good for learning), solid-color paper, or wrapping paper with a design only on one side. Be aware, though, that some kinds of paper stretch slightly, either in length or in width, while others tear easily.

Packets of papers especially for use in origami (15 by 15 centimeters square, or about 6 by 6 inches) are available in a variety of colors from craft and hobby shops. They may also carry origami paper in a larger size. You can, however, easily square off rectangular sheets, as shown on page 17, for projects of various sizes.

Regular typing paper may be too heavy to allow for the many tight folds needed in creating more complex, traditional origami figures, but it should be fine for several of the larger papercraft works, with fewer folds, given here. For those who are learning, and have a problem getting their fingers to work tight folds, larger paper sizes are fine. Slightly larger figures are easier to make than overly small ones.

Glue: Use a good, easy-flowing but not loose paper glue, but use it sparingly. You don't want to soak the paper. A flat toothpick makes a good applicator. Apply glue as needed then allow the glued form time to dry. Avoid using stick glue, as the application pressure needed (especially if the stick has become dry) can damage your figure.

Technique: Fold with care. Position the paper, especially at corners, precisely and see that edges line up before creasing a fold. Once you are sure of the fold, use a fingernail to make a clean, flat crease. Don't get discouraged with your first efforts. In time, what your mind can create, your fingers can fashion.

Symbols & Lines

Fold lines	valley	- - - - - - - - -	Fold then unfold		←——————→
	mountain	—·—·—·—·—			
Cut line		++++++++++++	Pleat fold (repeated folding)		———→
Turn over or rotate		⌒O⌒	Crease line		————

Basic Folds

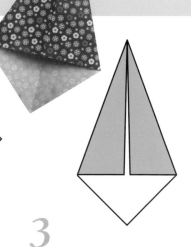

Kite Fold

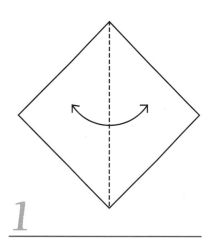
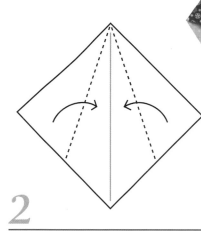

1
Fold and unfold a square diagonally, making a center crease.

2
Fold both sides in to the center crease.

3
This is a kite form.

Valley Fold   - - - - - - - - - - - - - -

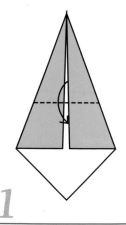
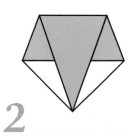

1
Here, using the kite, fold form toward you (forward), making a "valley."

2
This fold forward is a valley fold.

Mountain Fold   - · - · - · - · - · - ·

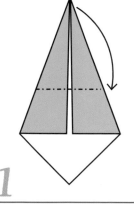
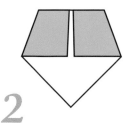

1
Here, using the kite, fold form away from you (backwards), making a "mountain."

2
This fold backwards is a mountain fold.

Inside Reverse Fold

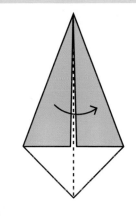

1
Starting here with a kite, valley fold kite closed.

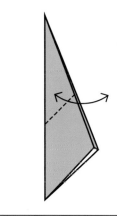

2
Valley fold as marked to crease, then unfold.

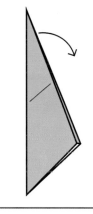

3
Pull tip in direction of arrow.

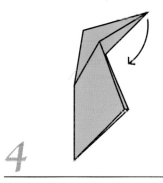

4
Appearance before completion.

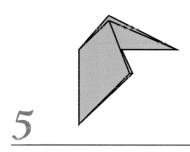

5
You've made an inside reverse fold.

Outside Reverse Fold

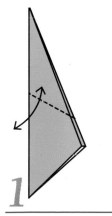

1
Using closed kite, valley fold, unfold.

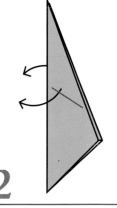

2
Fold inside out, as shown by arrows.

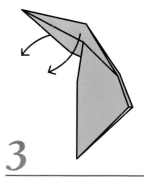

3
Appearance before completion.

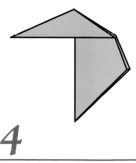

4
You've made an outside reverse fold.

Pleat Fold

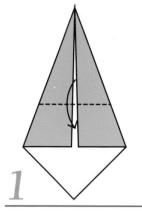 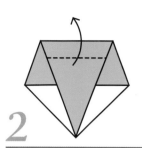 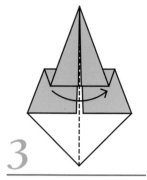 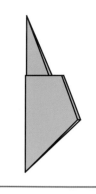

1 Here, using the kite, valley fold.

2 Valley fold back again.

3 This is a pleat. Valley fold in half.

4 You've made a pleat fold.

Pleat Fold Reverse

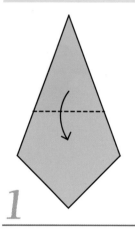 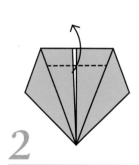 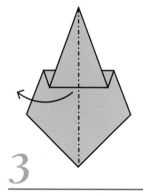 

1 Here, using the kite form backwards, valley fold.

2 Valley fold back again for pleat.

3 Mountain fold form in half.

4 This is a pleat fold reverse.

Squash Fold I

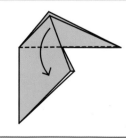 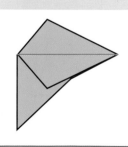

1 Using inside reverse, valley fold one side.

2 This is a squash fold I.

Squash Fold II

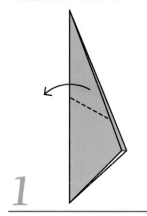

1

Using closed kite form, valley fold.

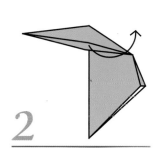

2

Open in direction of the arrow.

3

Appearance before completion.

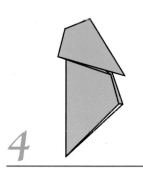

4

You've made a squash fold II.

Inside Crimp Fold

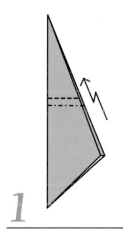

1

Here, using closed kite form, pleat fold.

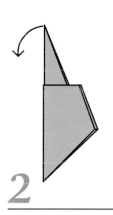

2

Pull tip in direction of the arrow.

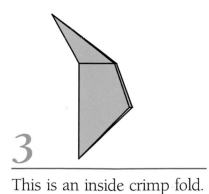

3

This is an inside crimp fold.

Outside Crimp Fold

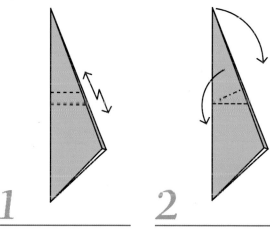

1

Here, using closed kite form, pleat fold and unfold.

2

Fold mountain and valley as shown, both sides.

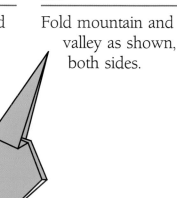

3

This is an outside crimp fold.

Basic Folds

Base Folds

Base folds are basic forms that do not in themselves produce origami, but serve as a basis, or jumping-off point, for a number of creative origami figures, some quite complex. As when beginning other crafts, learning to fold these base folds is not the most exciting part of origami. They are, however, easy to do, and will help you with your technique. They also quickly become rote, so much so that you can do many using different-colored papers while you are watching television or your mind is elsewhere. With completed base folds handy, if you want to quickly work up a form or are suddenly inspired with an idea for an original, unique figure, you can select an appropriate base fold and swiftly bring a new creation to life.

Base Fold I

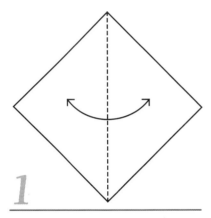

1

Fold and unfold in direction of arrow.

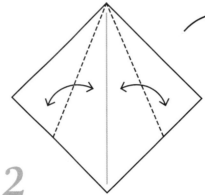

2

Fold both sides in to center crease, then unfold. Rotate.

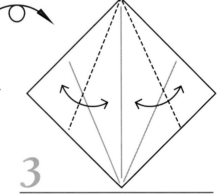

3

Fold both sides in to center crease, then unfold.

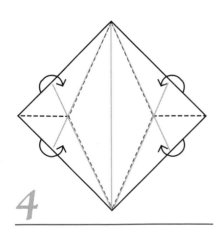

4

Pinch corners of square together and fold inward.

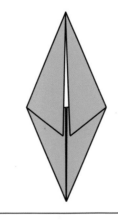

5

Completed Base Fold I.

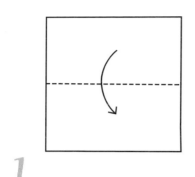

1

Valley fold.

2

Valley fold.

3

Squash fold.

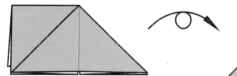

4

Turn over to other side.

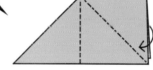

5

Squash fold.

6

Completed Base Fold II.

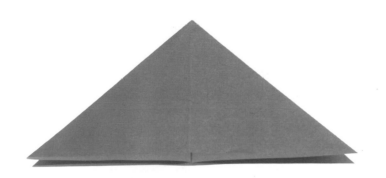

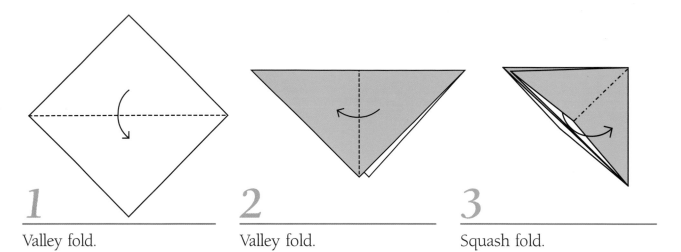

1   Valley fold.

2   Valley fold.

3   Squash fold.

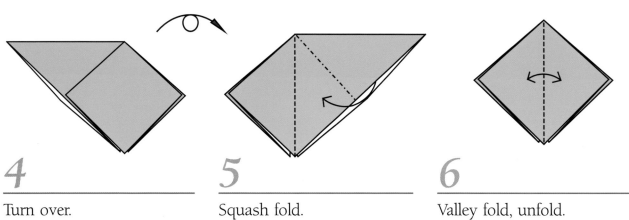

4   Turn over.

5   Squash fold.

6   Valley fold, unfold.

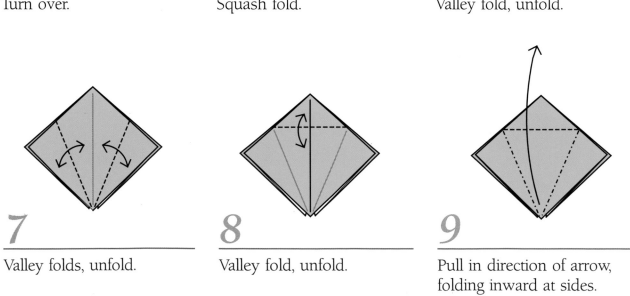

7   Valley folds, unfold.

8   Valley fold, unfold.

9   Pull in direction of arrow, folding inward at sides.

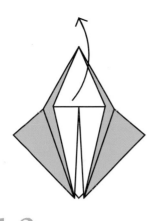

10

Appearance before
completion of fold.

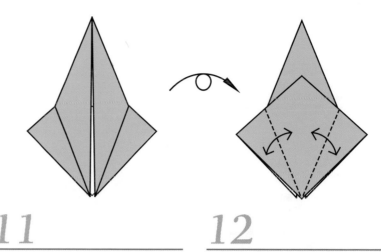

11

Fold completed. Turn over.

12

Valley folds, unfold.

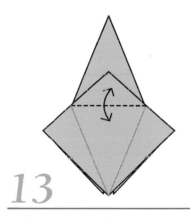

13

Valley fold, unfold.

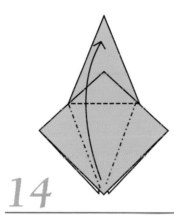

14

Repeat, again pulling in
direction of arrow.

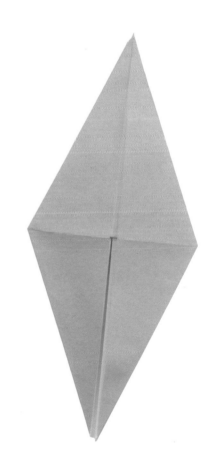

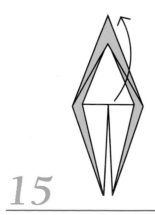

15

Appearance before
completion.

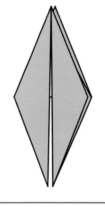

16

Completed Base Fold III.

Jack-o'-Lantern

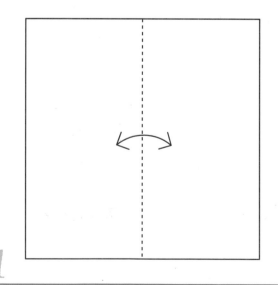

1

Valley fold then unfold.

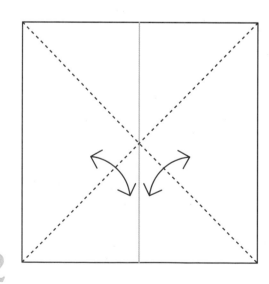

2

Valley folds then unfold, to crease.

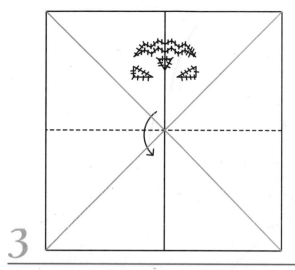

3

Make cuts (for face), then valley fold.

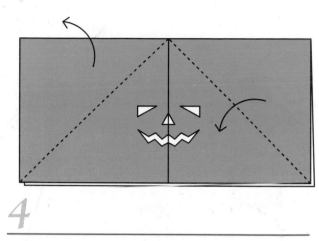

4

Mountain fold and valley fold.

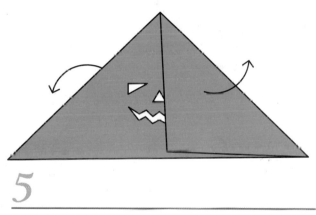

5

Unfolds.

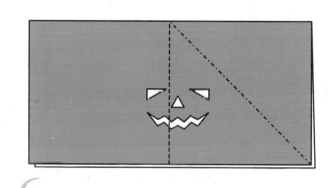

6

Squash fold.

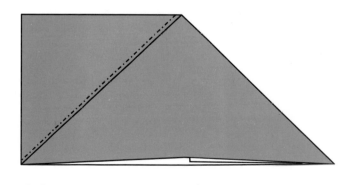

7

Repeat squash fold on back layer.

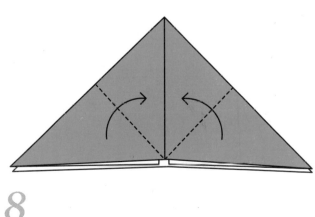

8

This is Base Fold II; now, valley folds.

Jack-o'-Lantern

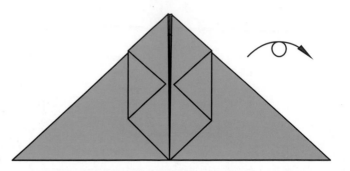

9

Valley folds.

10

Turn over.

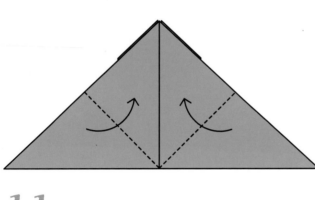

11

Valley folds. Look closer, now, at next steps.

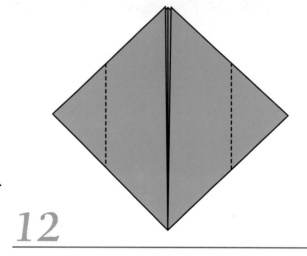

12

Valley folds, front and back.

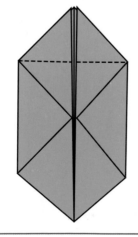

13

Valley folds, front and back.

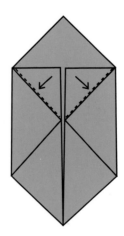

14

Valley and unfold front and back, then tuck flaps into pockets as shown.

Jack-o'-Lantern

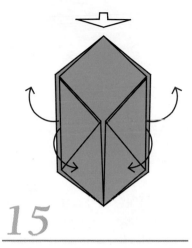

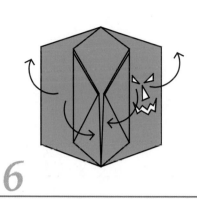

15

Push top down and pull open sides at same time.

16

Appearance before completion.

17

Completed Jack-o'-Lantern.

Squaring Off Paper

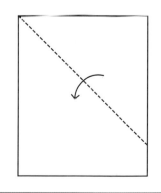

1

Take rectangular sheet, valley fold diagonally.

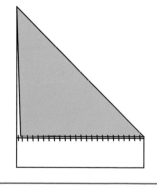

2

Cut off excess on long side as shown.

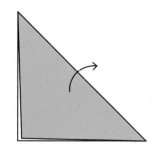

3

Unfold. Sheet is square, ready for any size form.

Jack-o'-Lantern

Scarecrow

Paper Usage page 21.

Part 1

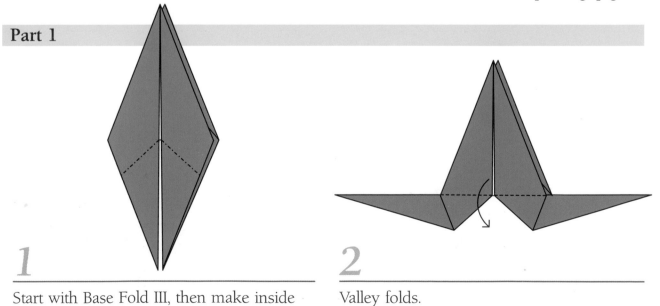

1

Start with Base Fold III, then make inside reverse folds.

2

Valley folds.

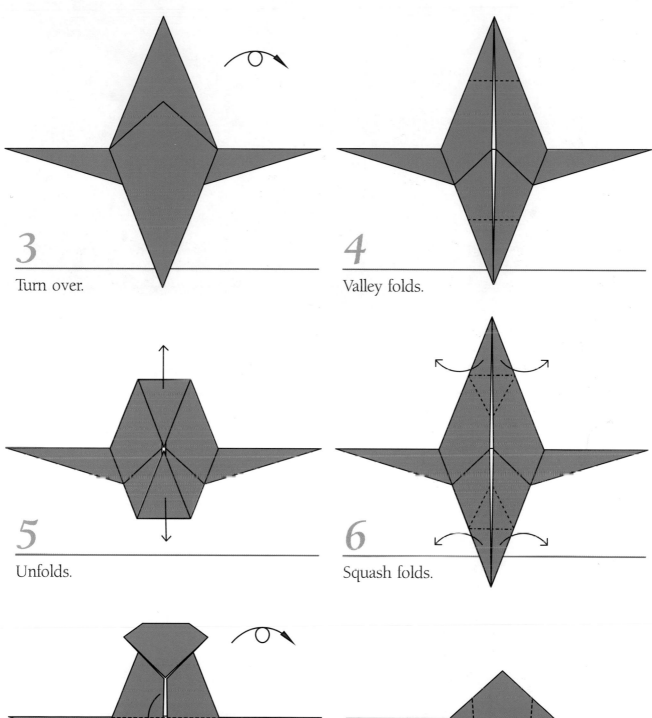

3
Turn over.

4
Valley folds.

5
Unfolds.

6
Squash folds.

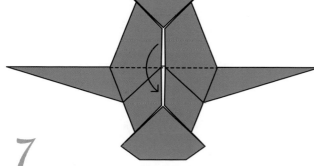

7
Valley folds front and back. Turn over.

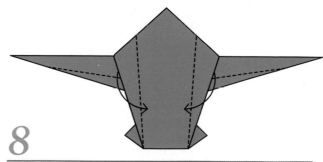

8
Valley and squash folds, front and back.

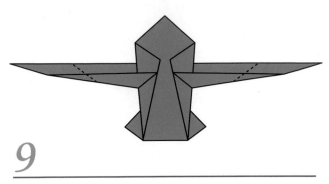

9

Valley folds, left and right.

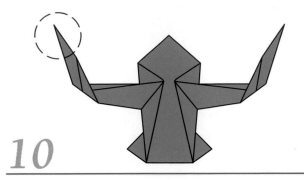

10

See close-up for details.

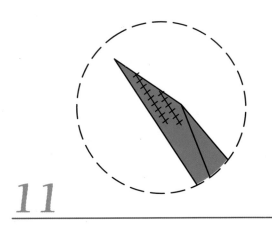

11

Make cuts as shown.

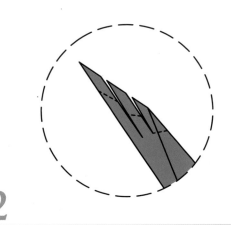

12

Valley folds top layer.

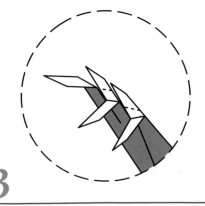

13

Valley folds second layer.

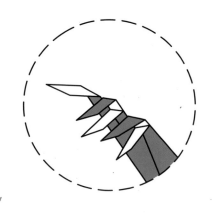

14

Return to full view.

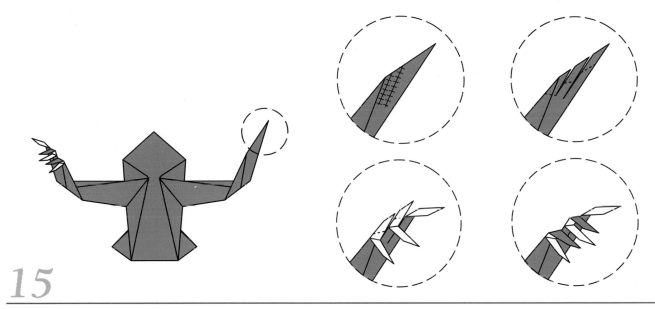

15

Repeat cuts and valley folds of separate layers on other side—mirror image.

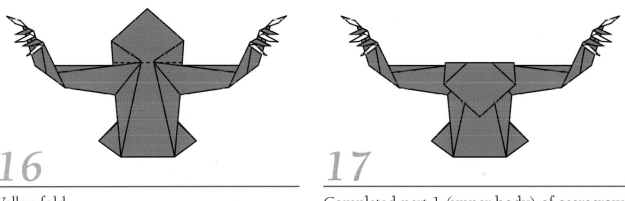

16

Valley fold.

17

Completed part 1 (upper body) of scarecrow.

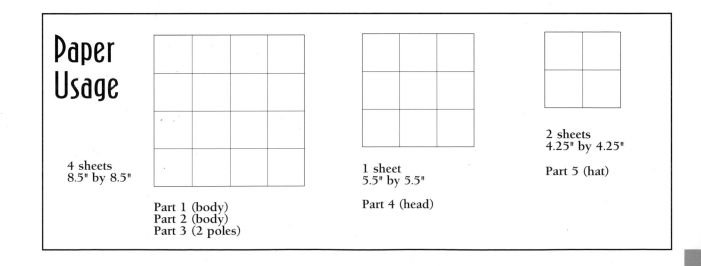

Paper Usage

4 sheets 8.5" by 8.5"

Part 1 (body)
Part 2 (body)
Part 3 (2 poles)

1 sheet 5.5" by 5.5"

Part 4 (head)

2 sheets 4.25" by 4.25"

Part 5 (hat)

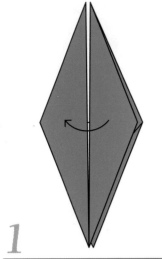

1

Start with Base Fold III.
Valley fold both sides.

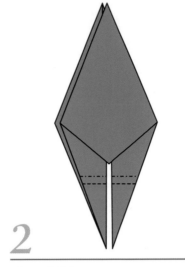

2

Pleat folds.

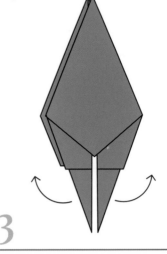

3

Pull in direction of arrows
and fold.

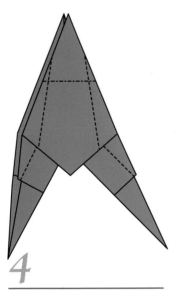

4

Valley fold the sides,
then mountain
fold top.

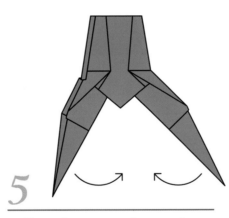

5

Pull as shown and squash
folds.

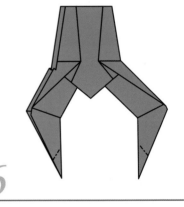

6

Inside reverse folds.

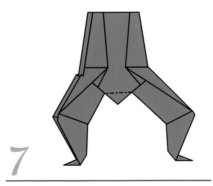

7

Mountain fold.

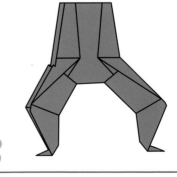

8

Completed part 2 (lower
body) of scarecrow.

Part 3

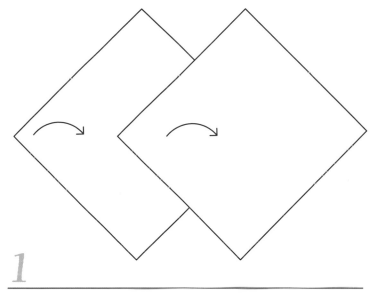

1

Roll two square sheets separately corner to corner, into tight mounting "poles" and glue. (Sipping straws may do for small scarecrow.)

2

Cross poles as shown and glue, for completed scarecrow mount.

Part 4

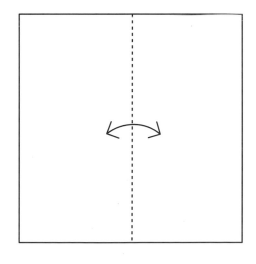

1

From square sheet, make jack-o'-lantern head (pages 14–17) to fit scarecrow.

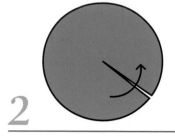

1
Make paper circle and cut as shown.

2
Pull to overlap slightly and apply glue to hold.

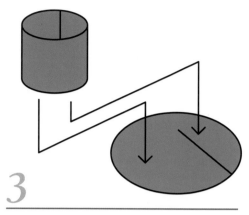

3
Cut second sheet in half and roll it into tube. Glue to hold, then glue edge to brim. (See pages 38–39 for another way to attach a hat crown to brim.)

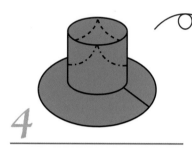

4
Mountain fold opposite sides of crown inward to touch. Rotate.

5
Completed part 5 (hat) of scarecrow, ready for decoration if desired.

To Attach

1
Join upper and lower body parts (parts 1 and 2).

Scarecrow

24

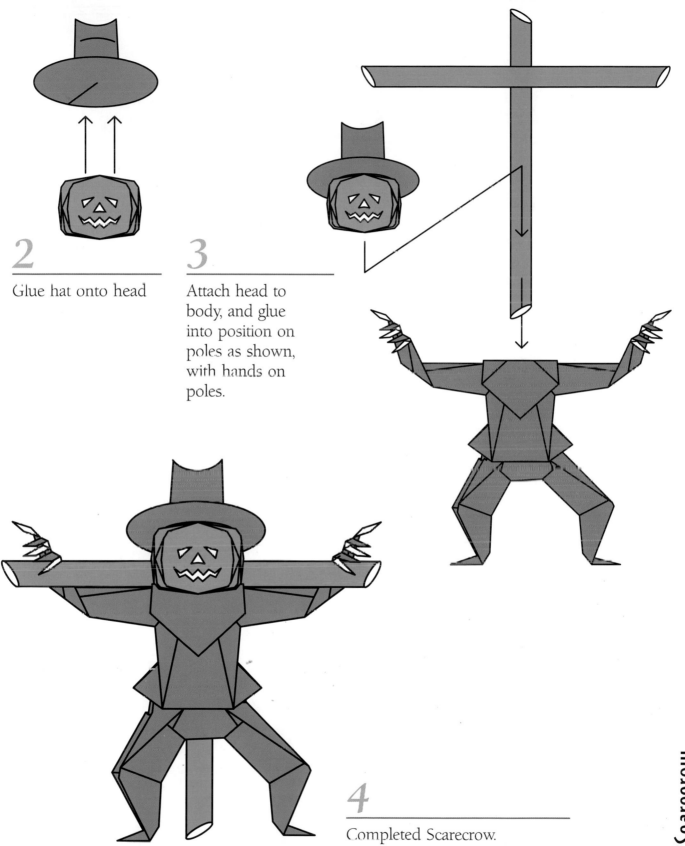

2

Glue hat onto head

3

Attach head to body, and glue into position on poles as shown, with hands on poles.

4

Completed Scarecrow.

Cat's Skull

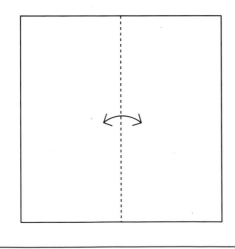

1

Valley fold and unfold.

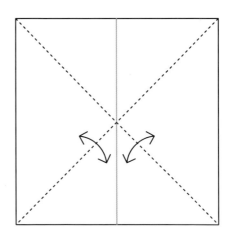

2

Valley fold then unfold.

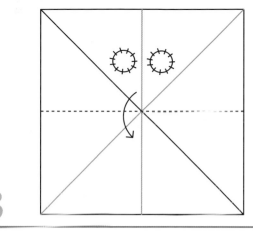

3

Cut out eyeholes, then valley fold.

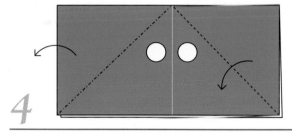

4

Mountain fold and valley fold.

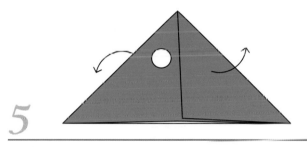

5

Unfold.

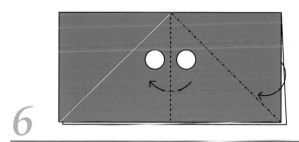

6

Squash fold.

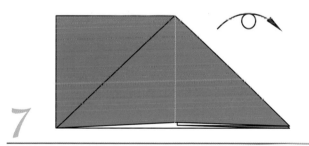

7

Turn over to other side.

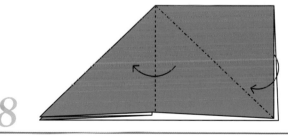

8

Squash fold.

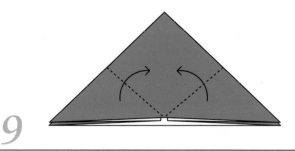

9

This is Base Fold II; now, valley folds.

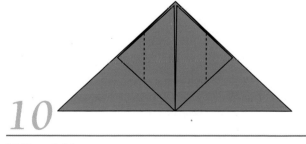

10

Valley folds.

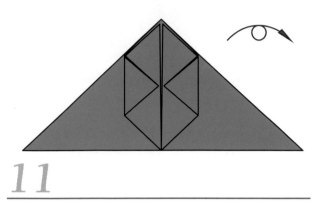

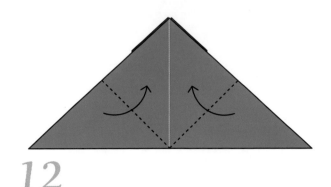

11

Turn over to other side.

12

Valley folds.

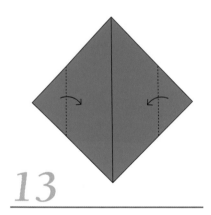

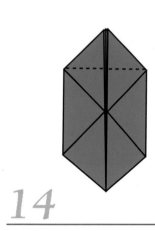

13

Valley folds.

14

Valley folds front and back.

15

Valley, unfold, then tuck flaps into pockets front and back.

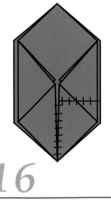

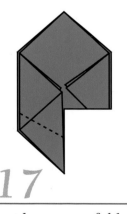

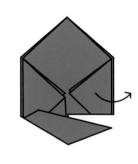

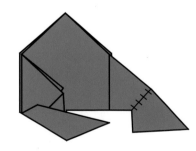

16

Cut through as shown.

17

Inside reverse fold.

18

Unfold.

19

Cut off section as shown.

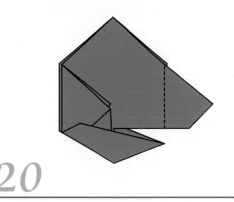

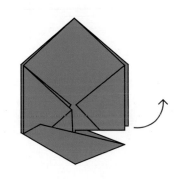

20

Valley fold both sides and glue down flaps.

21

Pull out.

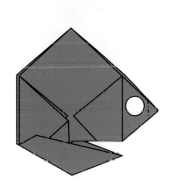

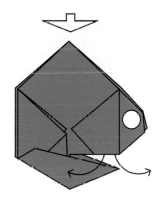

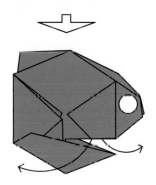

22

Inside reverse fold.

23

Push down on top, pull open at same time.

24

Opening out.

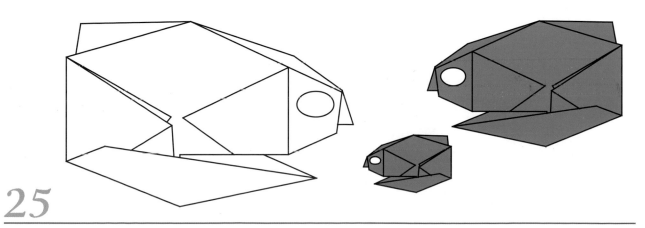

25

Completed Cat's Skull.

Grim Reaper

Paper Usage page 31.

Part 1

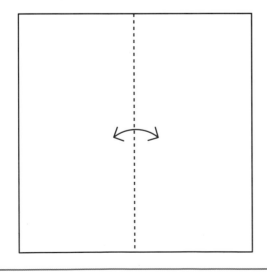

1

Valley fold then unfold.

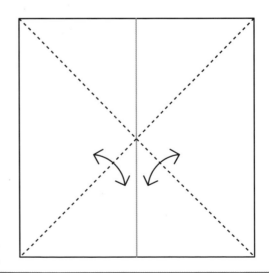

2

Valley fold then unfold.

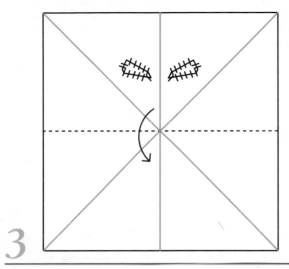

3

Cut out eyeholes, then valley fold.

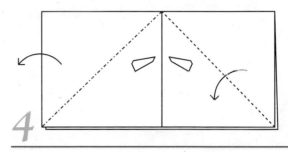

4

Mountain fold and valley fold.

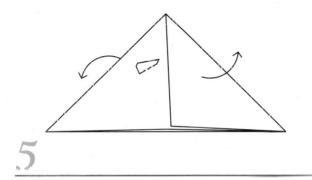

5

Unfold.

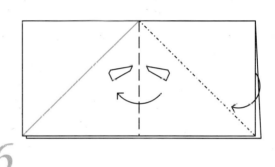

6

Squash fold.

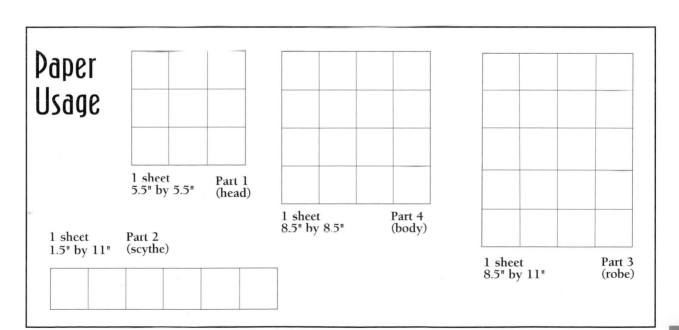

Paper Usage

1 sheet
5.5" by 5.5"   Part 1
                    (head)

1 sheet   Part 2
1.5" by 11"   (scythe)

1 sheet   Part 4
8.5" by 8.5"   (body)

1 sheet   Part 3
8.5" by 11"   (robe)

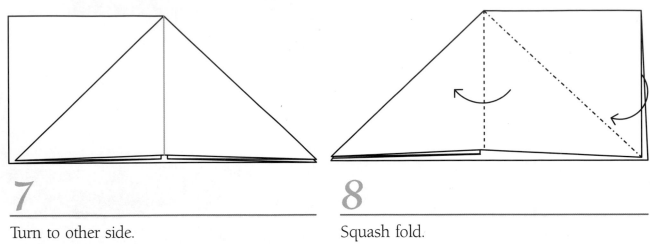

7

Turn to other side.

8

Squash fold.

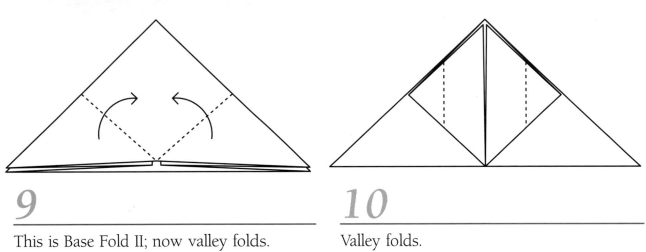

9

This is Base Fold II; now valley folds.

10

Valley folds.

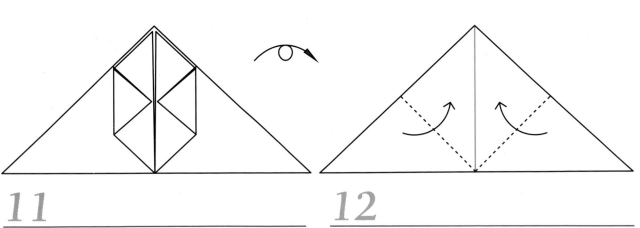

11

Turn to other side.

12

Valley folds.

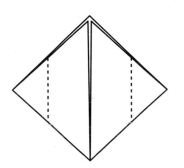

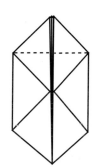

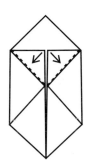

13

Valley folds, front and back.

14

Valley fold front and back.

15

Valley and unfold, then tuck flaps into pockets.

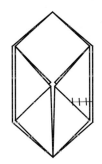

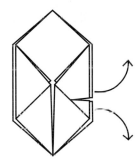

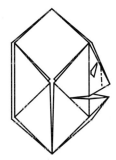

16

Cut as shown, deeper into hidden inner fold.

17

Pull cut top layer outward to form face.

18

Inside reverse fold.

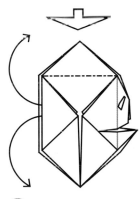

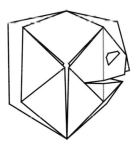

19

Push down on top and pull open.

20

Completed part 1 (head) of Grim Reaper.

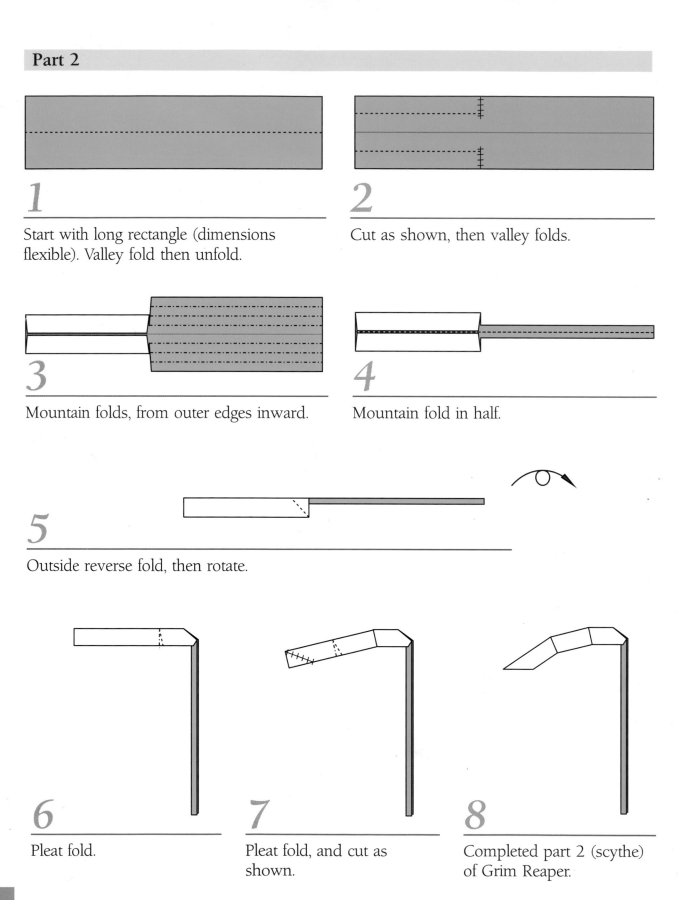

1

Start with long rectangle (dimensions flexible). Valley fold then unfold.

2

Cut as shown, then valley folds.

3

Mountain folds, from outer edges inward.

4

Mountain fold in half.

5

Outside reverse fold, then rotate.

6

Pleat fold.

7

Pleat fold, and cut as shown.

8

Completed part 2 (scythe) of Grim Reaper.

Grim Reaper

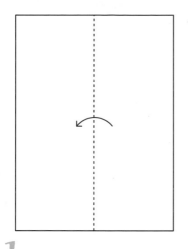

1
Valley fold.

2
Squash fold.

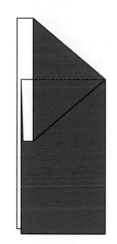

3
Mountain folds.

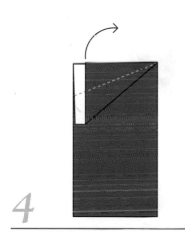

4
Pull and fold.

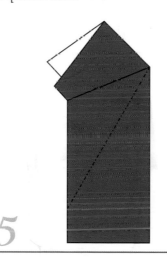

5
Inside reverse fold.

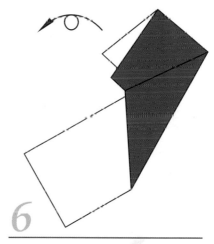

6
Rotate to upright.

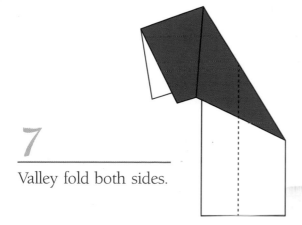

7
Valley fold both sides.

8
Completed part 3 (upper body) of Grim Reaper.

Grim Reaper

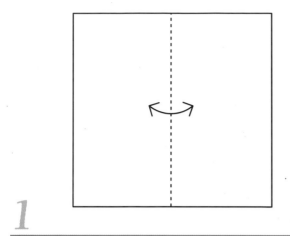

1

Valley fold and unfold for center crease.

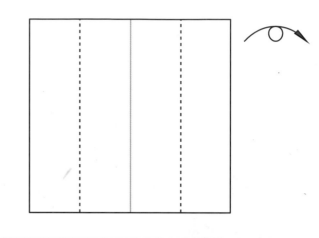

2

Valley fold both sides to center. Turn over.

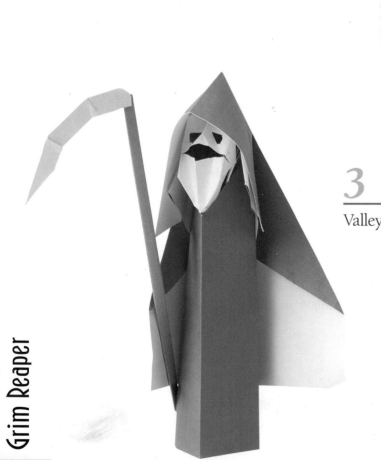

3

Valley folds.

4

Mountain fold in half.

5

Completed part 4 (lower body) of Grim Reaper.

Grim Reaper

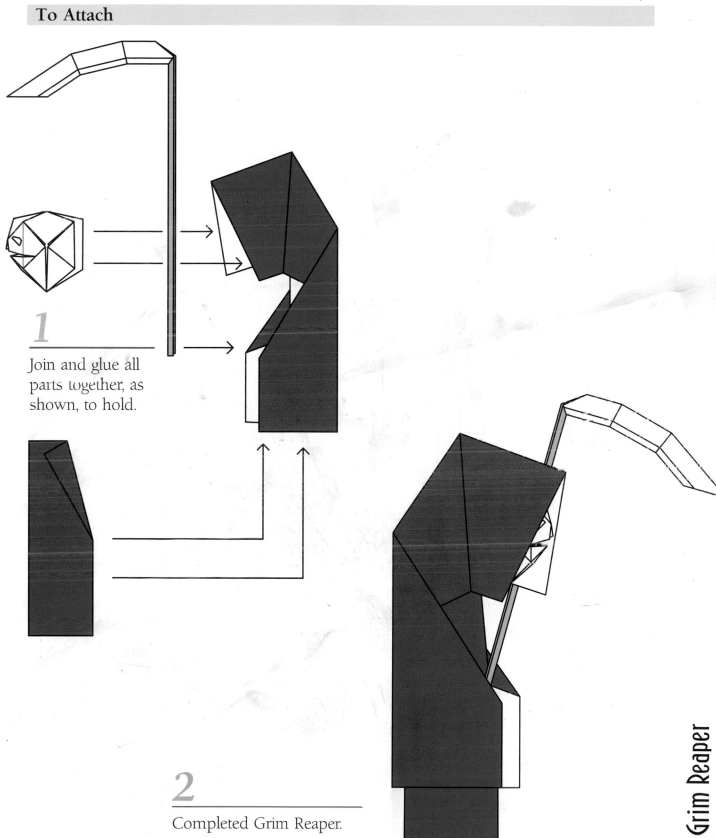

1

Join and glue all parts together, as shown, to hold.

2

Completed Grim Reaper.

Grim Reaper

Witch

Paper Usage page 42.

Part 1

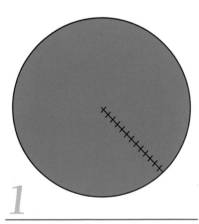

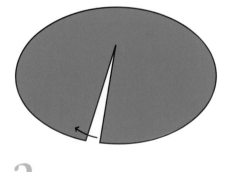

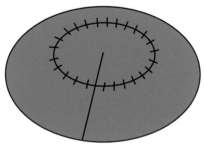

1
Place round item on sheet for circle, then cut as shown.

2
Pull in direction of arrow for hat brim.

3
Glue in place, then cut central opening as shown.

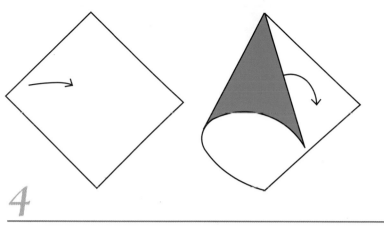

4

Roll tip of another sheet to form cone.

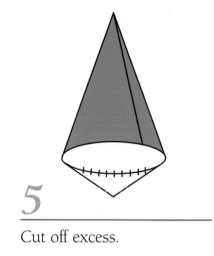

5

Cut off excess.

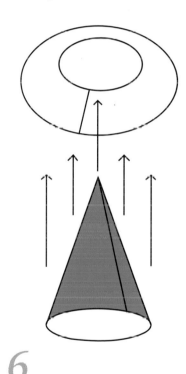

6

Join by passing hat top up into brim.

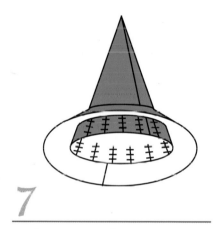

7

Make cuts as shown.

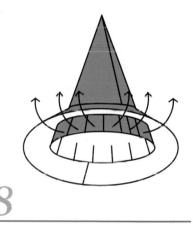

8

Valley fold flaps up and glue.

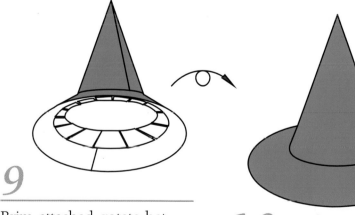

9

Brim attached, rotate hat.

10

Completed part 1 (hat) of witch.

Witch

39

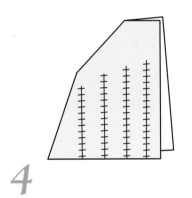

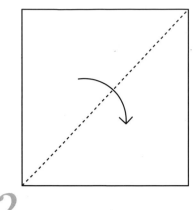

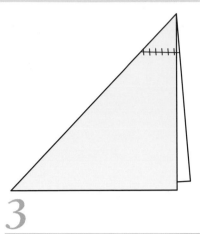

1

From square, make cat's skull (pages 26–29).

2

For hair, valley fold another square.

3

Cut as shown.

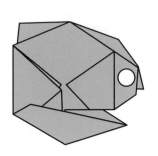

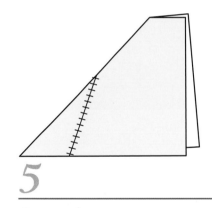

4

Cut as shown.

5

Cut as shown.

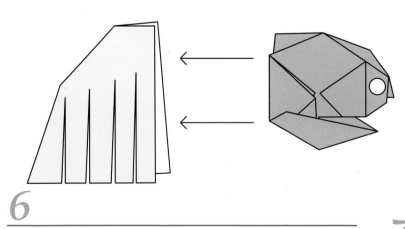

6

Glue skull and hair together.

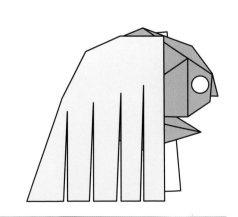

7

Completed part 2 (head) of witch.

Witch

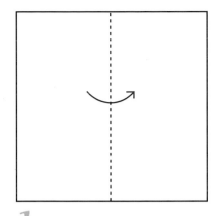

1

Valley fold in half.

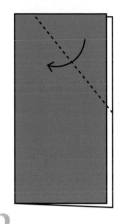

2

Valley fold both layers
together, apply glue to hold.

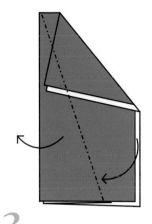

3

Open out and squash fold.

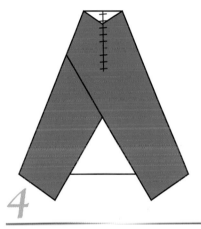

4

Cut through, then unfold.

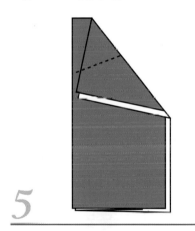

5

Valley fold.

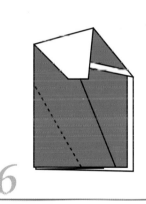

6

Inside reverse fold.

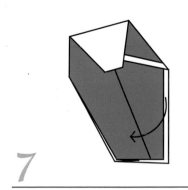

7

Pull open at creases.

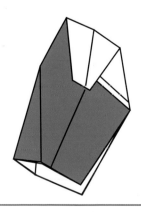

8

Completed part 3 (cape) of witch.

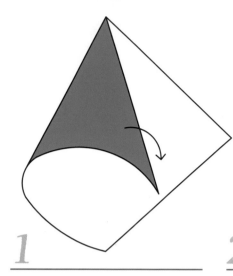

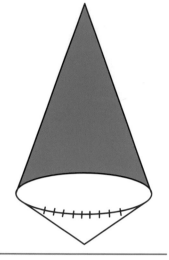

1
Roll sheet into cone, glue.

2
Trim off excess.

3
Completed part 4 (body) of witch.

Paper Usage

3 sheets
4.25" by 4.25"

Part 1 (hat brim)
Part 1 (hat crown)
Part 2 (hair)

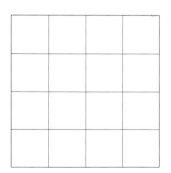

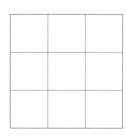

2 sheets   Part 3 (cape)
8.5" by 8.5"   Part 4 (body)

1 sheet
5.5" by 5.5"

Part 2 (skull)

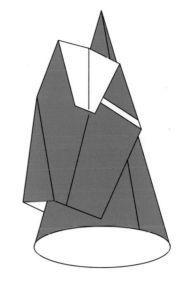

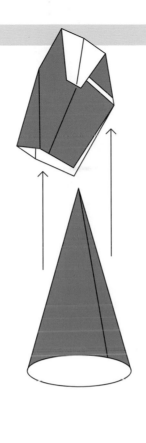

1

Place part 3 (cape) over part 4 (body). Glue to hold.

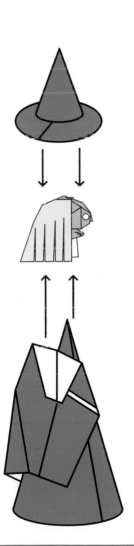

2

Assemble hat, head, and caped body as shown. Glue to hold.

3

Completed Witch.

Witch

43

Gremlin Mask

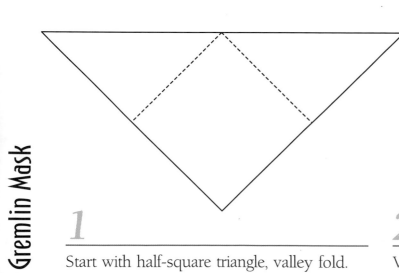

1

Start with half-square triangle, valley fold.

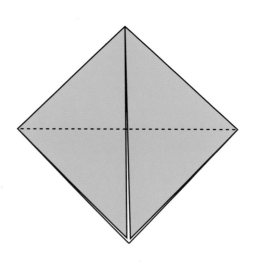

2

Valley folds.

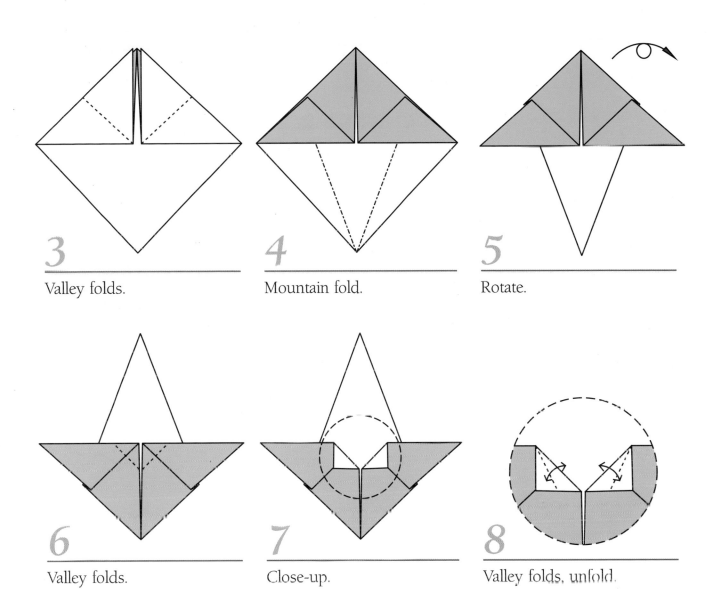

3

Valley folds.

4

Mountain fold.

5

Rotate.

6

Valley folds.

7

Close-up.

8

Valley folds, unfold.

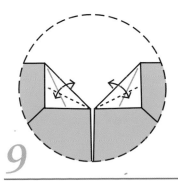

9

Valley folds, unfold.

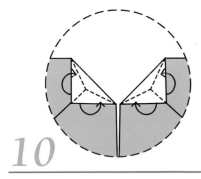

10

Pinch together at corners, and valley fold inward.

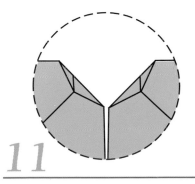

11

Back to full view.

Gremlin Mask

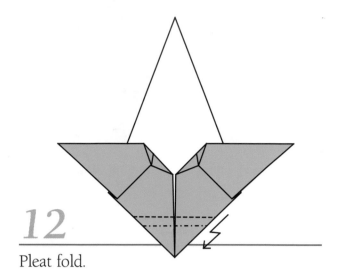

12

Pleat fold.

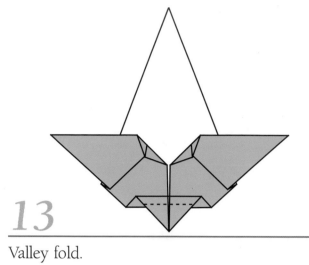

13

Valley fold.

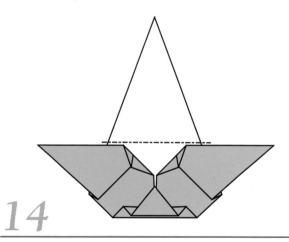

14

Mountain fold.

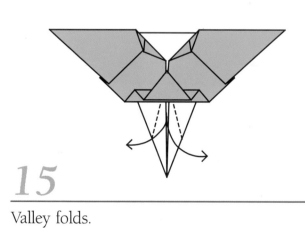

15

Valley folds.

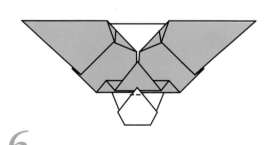

16

Valley fold tip.

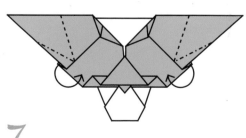

17

Valley folds and squash folds.

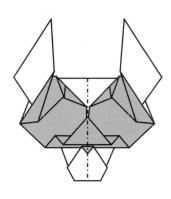

18

Mountain fold in half.

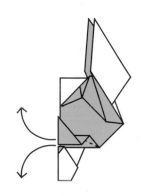

19

Pull and crimp fold.

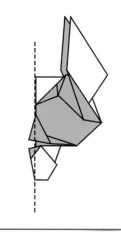

20

Open out folds.

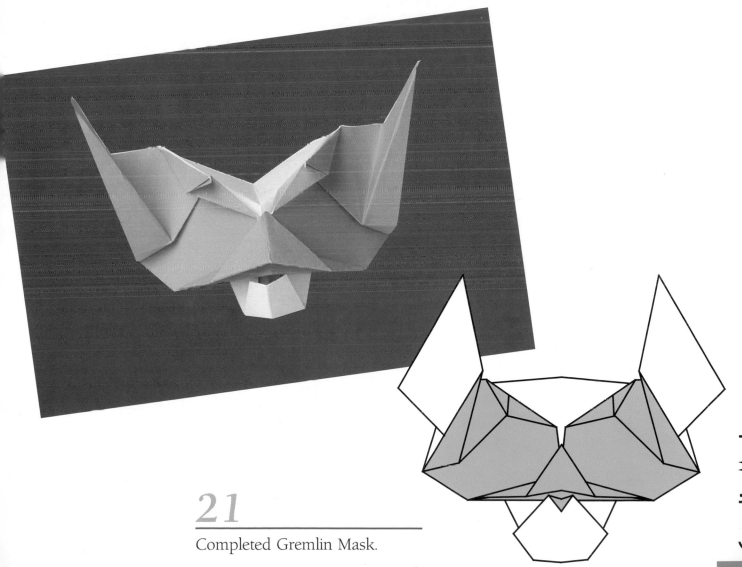

21

Completed Gremlin Mask.

Angel

Paper Usage page 51.

Paper Usage page 51.

Part 1

1

Valley fold sheet as shown, in thirds.

2

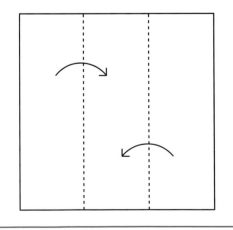

Apply glue to lower inside front layer only.

3

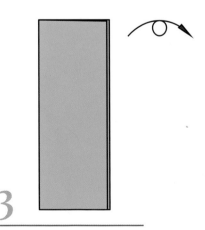

Turn over.

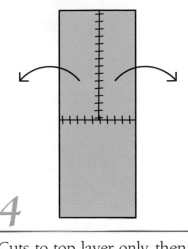

4

Cuts to top layer only, then open out to sides.

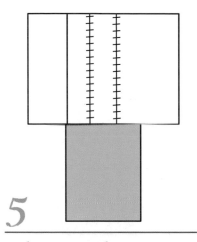

5

Make cuts as shown.

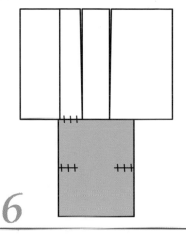

6

Cut and remove top strip. Make side cuts through.

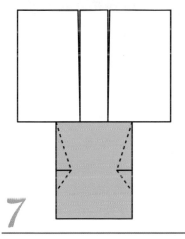

7

Valley fold side sections.

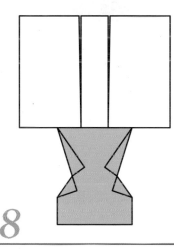

8

Apply glue to side folds.

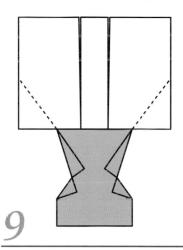

9

Valley folds.

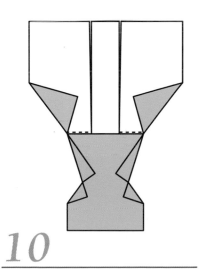

10

Valley folds.

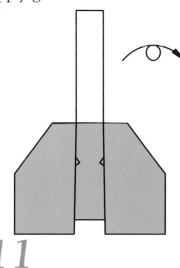

11

Turn over to other side.

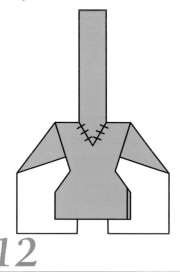

12

Cut front layer and discard.

Angel

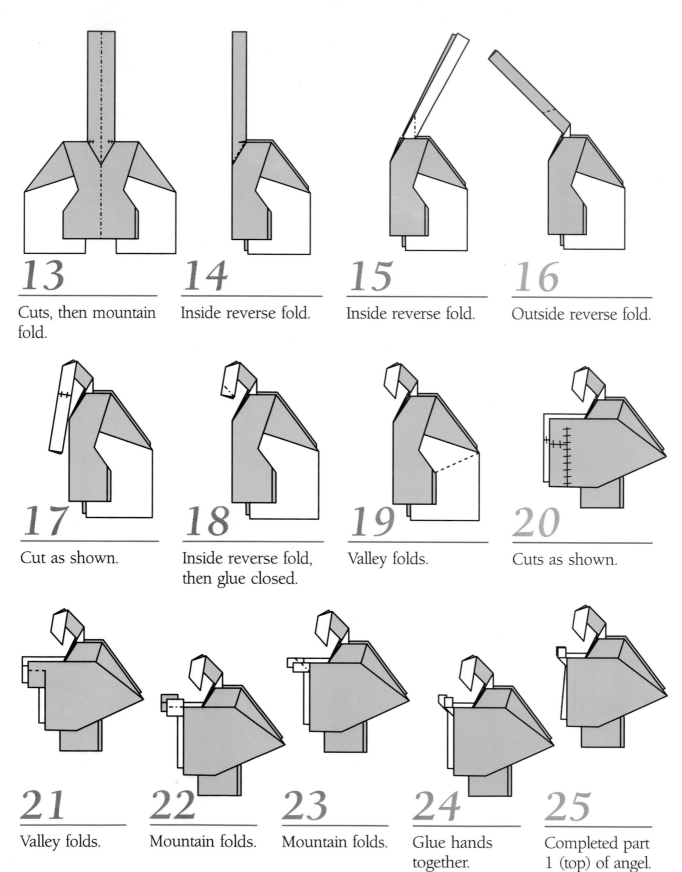

13
Cuts, then mountain fold.

14
Inside reverse fold.

15
Inside reverse fold.

16
Outside reverse fold.

17
Cut as shown.

18
Inside reverse fold, then glue closed.

19
Valley folds.

20
Cuts as shown.

21
Valley folds.

22
Mountain folds.

23
Mountain folds.

24
Glue hands together.

25
Completed part 1 (top) of angel.

Part 2

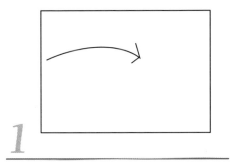

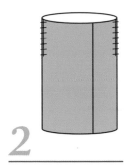

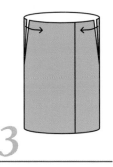

1
Roll into tube shape to fit inside angel top, and glue.

2
Cuts as shown.

3
Taper both sides and glue.

4
Completed part 2 (lower body) of angel.

Part 3

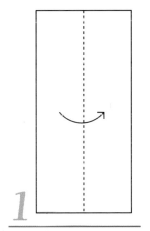

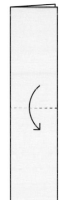

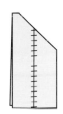

1
Valley fold strip.

2
Valley fold.

3
Inside reverse fold.

4
Cut off as shown.

5
Completed part 3 (hair) of angel.

Paper Usage

1 sheet 8.5" by 8.5"

Part 1 (top body)

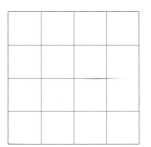

1 sheet 2" by 6"

Part 3 (hair)

1 sheet 8.5" by 5"

Part 2 (lower body)

1 sheet 4" by 12"

Part 4 (wings)

Angel

Part 4

1

Start with strip of paper, valley fold.

2

Valley fold, then rotate.

3

Valley fold.

4

Squash fold.

5

Mountain fold.

6

Cut as shown.

7

Valley fold both sides.

8

Valley fold both sides.

9

Cuts as shown.

10

Unfold, to open out wings.

11

Make cuts.

12

Completed part 4 (wings) of angel.

Angel

To Attach

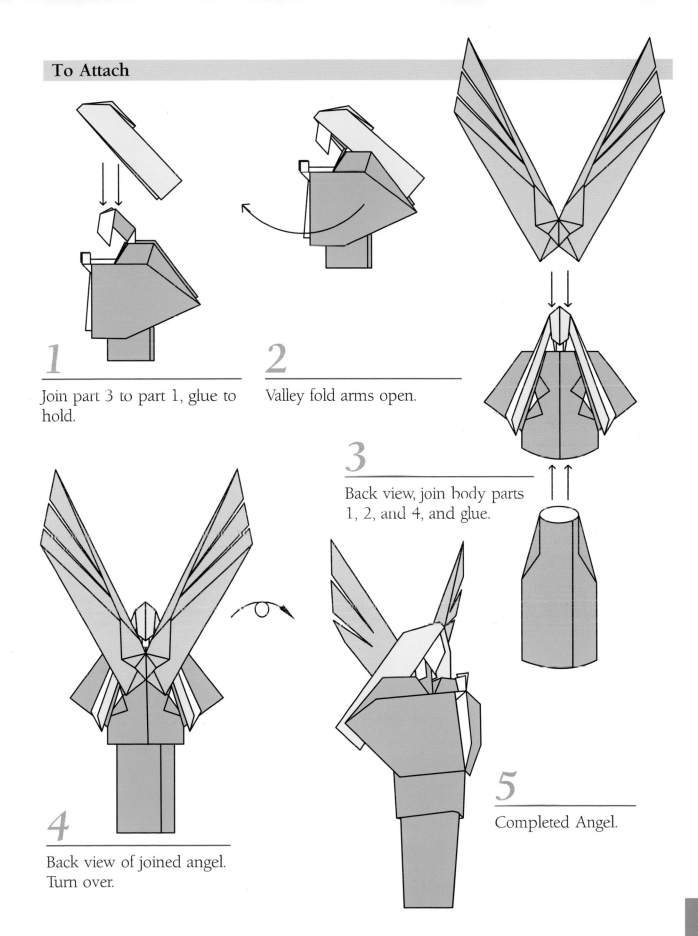

1

Join part 3 to part 1, glue to hold.

2

Valley fold arms open.

3

Back view, join body parts 1, 2, and 4, and glue.

4

Back view of joined angel. Turn over.

5

Completed Angel.

Snowman

Part 1

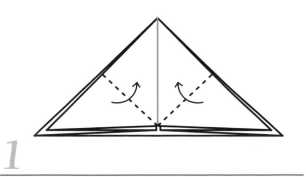

1 Using Base Fold II, valley fold sides to center crease.

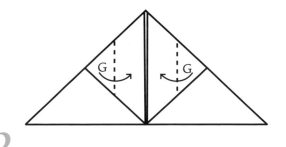

2 Apply glue (G) to triangles, then valley fold.

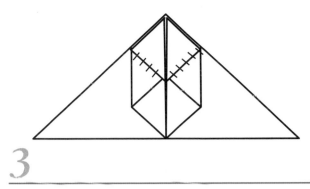

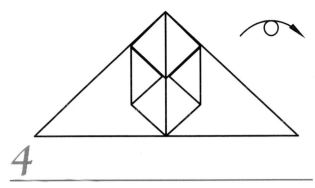

3

Make cuts to top layer as shown, and discard the two upper triangles.

4

Turn over to other side.

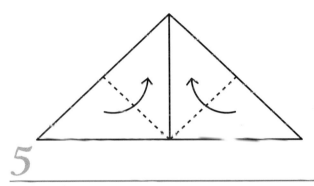

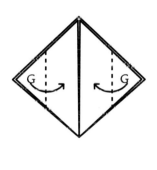

5

Again, valley folds to center crease.

6

Apply glue, then valley fold.

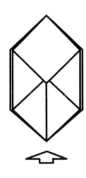

7

Make cuts to the top layer and discard triangles.

8

Blow into bottom center opening and pull form open, to inflate and form box.

9

Part 1 (bottom body) of snowman.

Parts 2 and 3

1
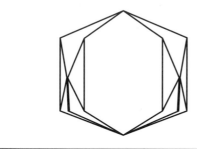
For part 2 (top body), make part 1 in smaller size.

2
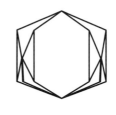
For part 3 (head), make part 1 in even smaller size.

Part 4

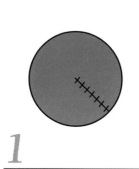  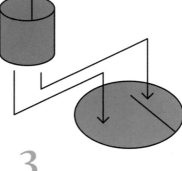 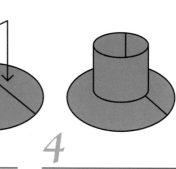

1
Make paper circle and cut as shown.

2
Pull as shown and apply glue to hold brim.

3
Form paper tube, add glue to edge and attach to brim.

4
Completed part 4 (hat) of snowman.

Part 5

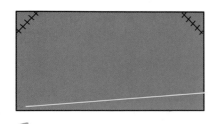 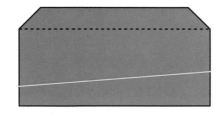 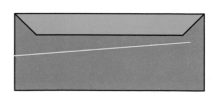

1
Start with rectangle of paper, make cuts as shown.

2
Valley fold.

3
Completed part 5 (cape) of snowman.

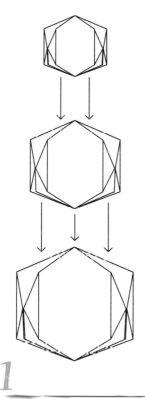

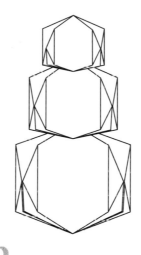

1

Build snowman,
gluing parts 1, 2, and
3 together to hold.

2

Basic snowman ready
for hat and cape.

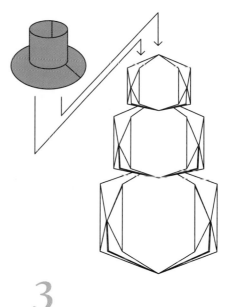

3

Glue hat to head
of snowman.

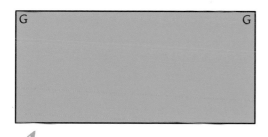

4

Wrap cape around snowman.
Glue at top corners, inside
collar, to hold.

5

Completed basic
Snowman. Add
paper-coal eyes,
carrot nose, and
mouth.

Other decoration
ideas: corncob pipe,
scarf, buttons, bow tie.

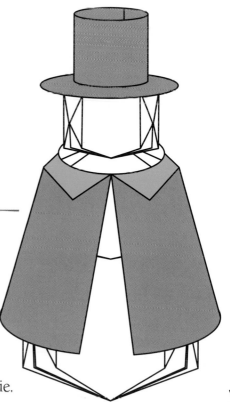

Snowman

Kris Kringle

Paper Usage page 65.

Part 1

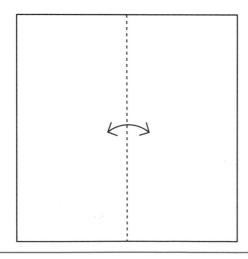

1 Valley fold then unfold.

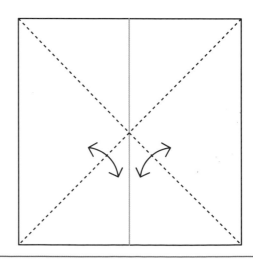

2 Valley folds then unfold.

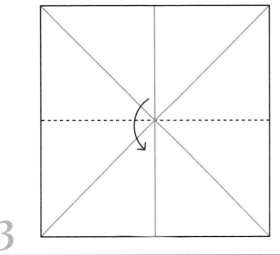

3

Valley fold.

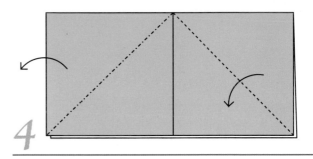

4

Mountain and valley fold.

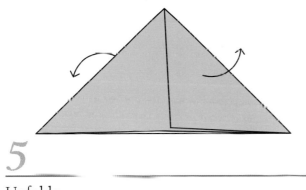

5

Unfolds.

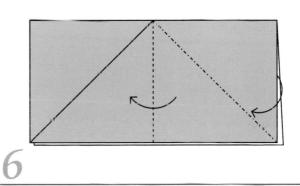

6

Squash fold.

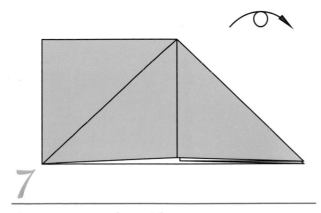

7

Turn over to other side.

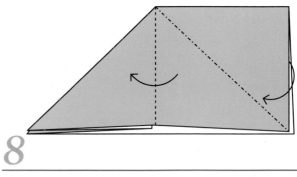

8

Squash fold.

Kris Kringle

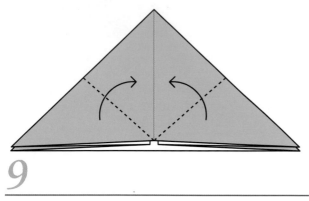

9

This is Base Fold II; now, valley folds.

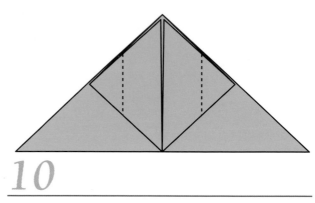

10

Valley folds.

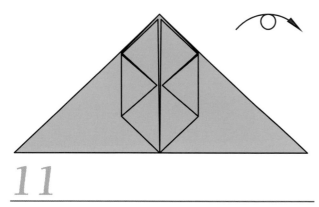

11

Turn over to other side.

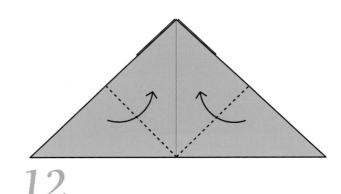

12

Valley folds.

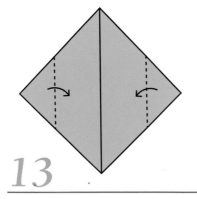

13

Valley folds.

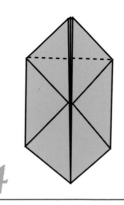

14

Valley folds, front and back.

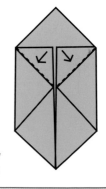

15

Valley and unfold, then tuck flaps into pockets as shown, front and back.

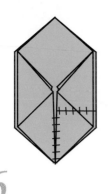

16

Cut through layers as shown.

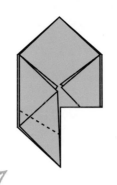

17

Outside reverse fold, both sides.

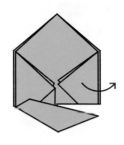

18

Unfold both sides.

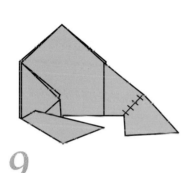

19

Cut through as shown.

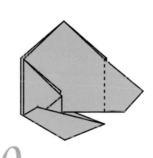

20

Valley fold and glue both sides to hold.

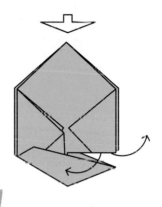

21

Push top down and open out.

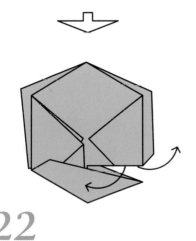

22

Appearance before completion.

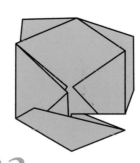

23

Completed part 1 (head) of Kris Kringle.

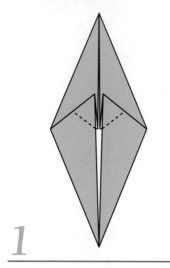

1

Start with Base Fold I, then valley folds.

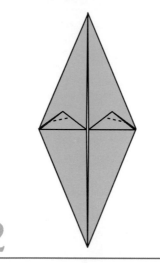

2

Inside reverse folds.

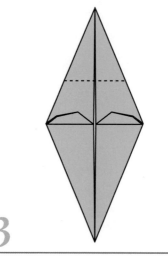

3

Valley fold.

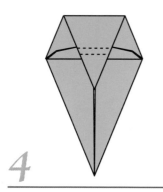

4

Pleat fold.

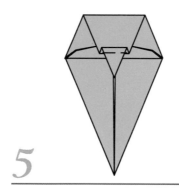

5

Valley fold.

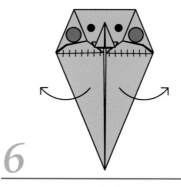

6

Draw eyes and cheeks, then cut and unfold.

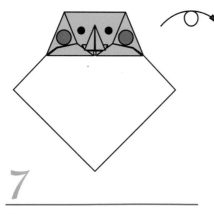

7

Turn over.

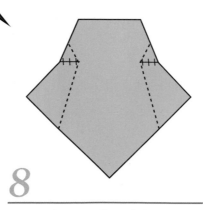

8

Cuts, then valley folds.

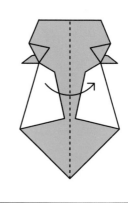

9

Valley fold in half.

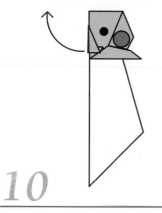

10

Pull face outward slightly and squash fold.

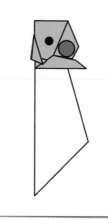

11

Open out.

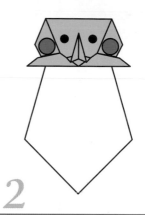

12

Completed part 2 (face) of Kris Kringle.

Part 3

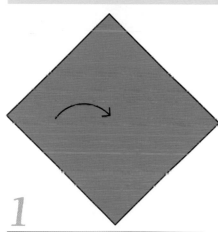

1

Roll corner of square sheet in direction of arrow.

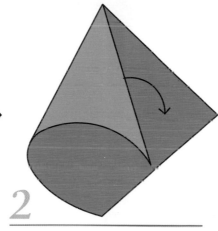

2

Form into cone and glue to hold.

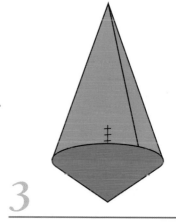

3

Cut as shown.

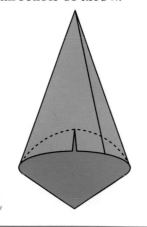

4

Valley folds.

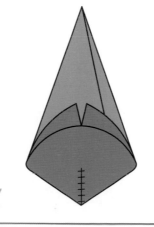

5

Cut as shown.

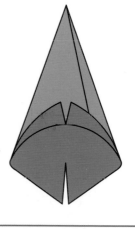

6

Completed part 3 (hat) of Kris Kringle.

Kris Kringle

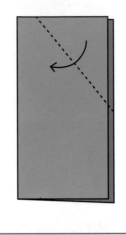

1
Valley fold in half.

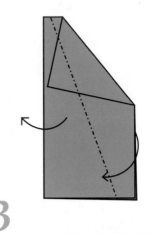

2
Valley fold layers together and apply glue to hold.

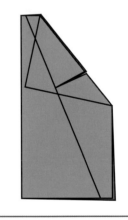

3
Open form and squash fold.

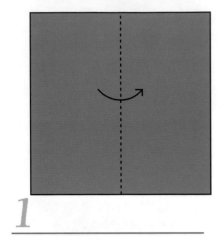

4
Cut top layer only, and return to previous position.

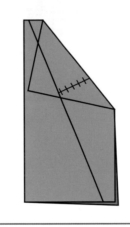

5
Cut through as shown.

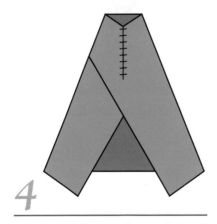

6
Squash fold open again.

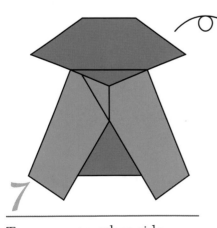

7
Turn over to other side.

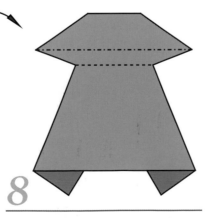

8
Pleat fold.

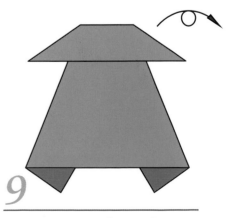

9
Turn over to other side.

Kris Kringle

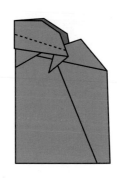

10
Valley folds, tucking flaps behind form.

11
Squash fold to side view.

12
Outside reverse fold.

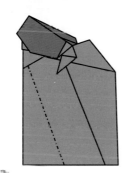

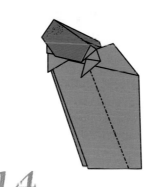

13
Inside reverse fold.

14
Squash fold to front view.

15
Complete part 4 (top body) of Kris Kringle.

Paper Usage

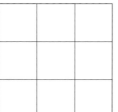

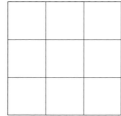

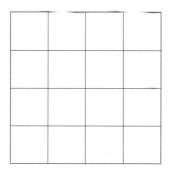

1 sheet
2.25" by 2.25"

Part 2 (face)

1 sheet
5.5" by 5.5"

Part 1 (head)

1 sheet
4.25" by 4.25"

Part 3 (hat)

2 sheets   Part 4 (robe)
8.5" by 8.5"   Part 5 (body)

Kris Kringle

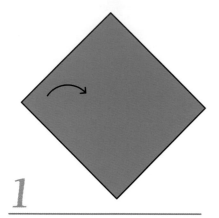

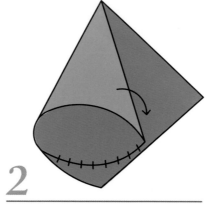

1 Roll square sheet in direction of arrow.

2 Form into cone, glue to hold. Cut off excess.

3 Completed part 5 (body base) of Kris Kringle.

To Attach

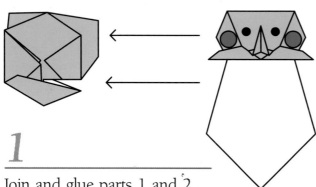

1 Join and glue parts 1 and 2 (head) together as shown.

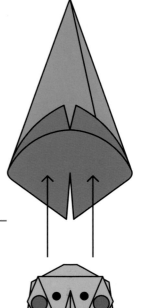

2 Add part 3 (hat) and glue to hold.

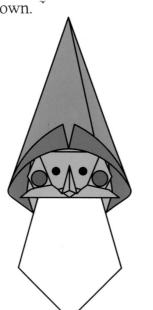

3 Completed head of Kris Kringle.

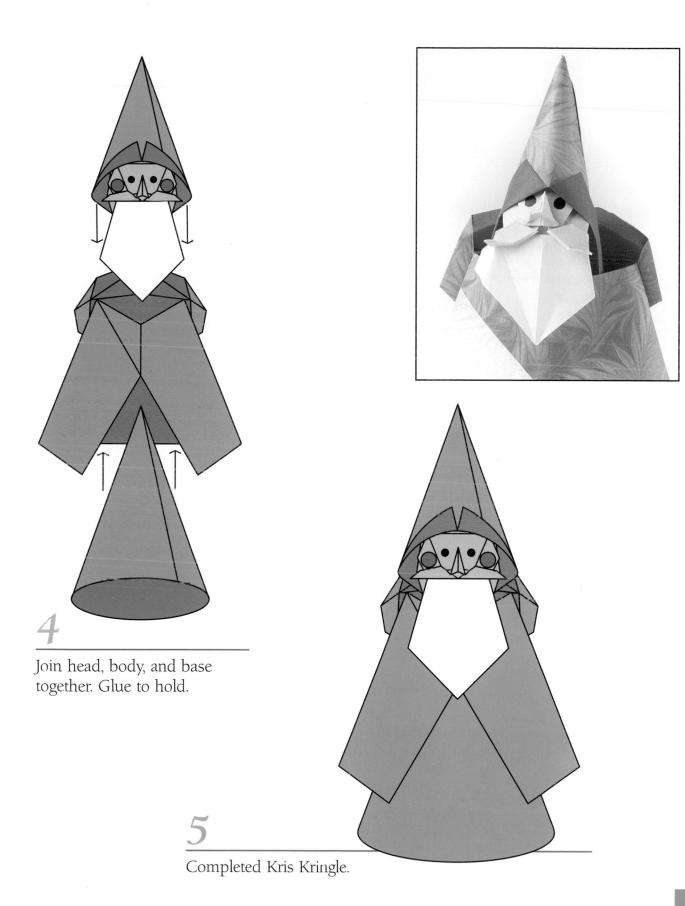

4

Join head, body, and base together. Glue to hold.

5

Completed Kris Kringle.

Santa Claus

Paper Usage page 73.

Part 1

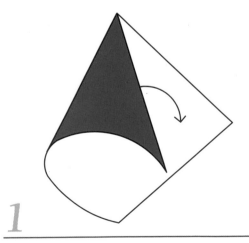

1
Roll square into cone, and glue.

2
Cut off excess.

3
Top part of hat.

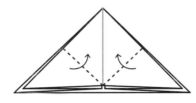

4

Start with paper strip, valley fold.

5

Fit opening of folded strip over cone end (see next step).

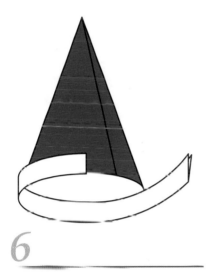

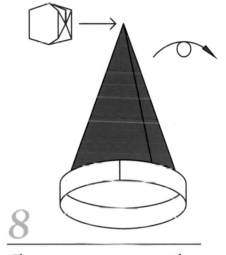

6

Wrap completely around cone end. Apply glue as you go.

7

Using small size Base Fold II, form pompom (see snowman pages 54–55).

8

Glue pompom to one side of tip of hat. Rotate.

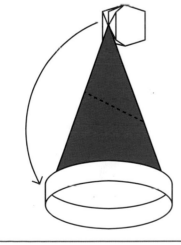

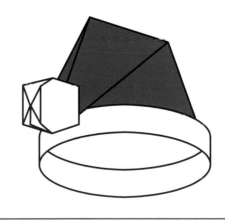

9

Valley fold to one side as shown, glue to hold pompom in position.

10

Completed part 1 (hat) of Santa Claus. (A large-sized hat makes a cute decoration in itself!)

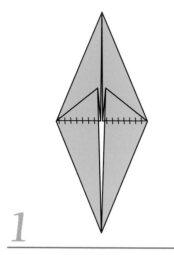

1

Start with Base Fold I, cut top layer only as shown.

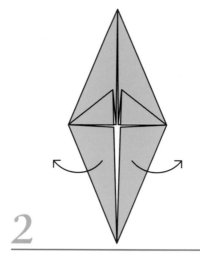

2

Unfolds.

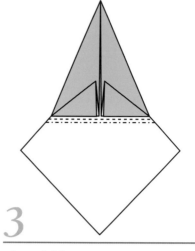

3

Pleat fold.

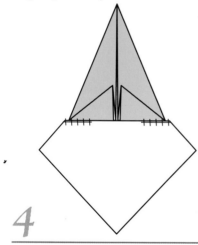

4

Cuts as shown.

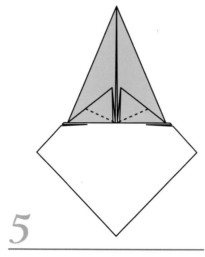

5

Valley folds.

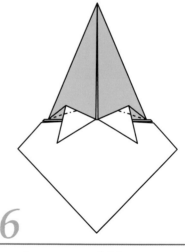

6

Inside reverse folds.

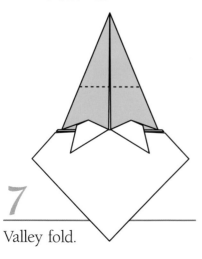

7

Valley fold.

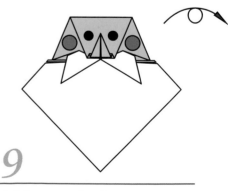

8

Pleat fold.

9

Add eyes, cheeks. Turn over.

Santa Claus

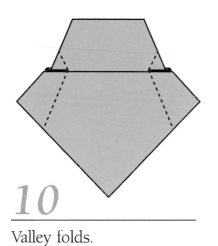

10

Valley folds.

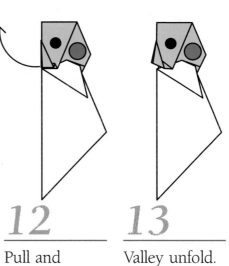

11

Valley fold in half.

12

Pull and crimp fold.

13

Valley unfold.

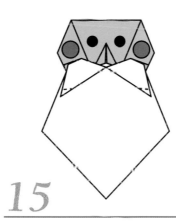

14

Tuck face section behind mustache.

15

Valley folds.

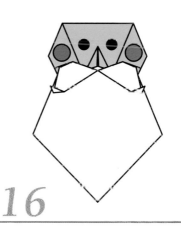

16

Completed face section, for head.

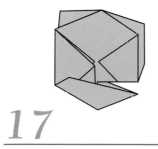

17

Make head from new square (see Kris Kringle, pages 58–61).

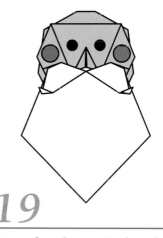

18

Attach Santa face to head.

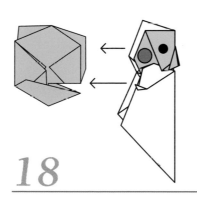

19

Completed part 2 (head) of Santa Claus.

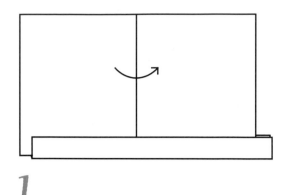

1

Valley fold strip to fit over sheet as shown, valley fold in half.

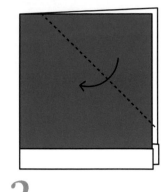

2

Valley fold both layers.

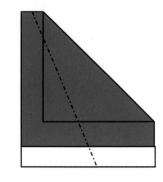

3

Glue and squash fold to open out front.

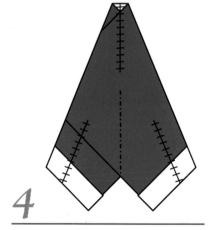

4

Cut as shown, then return to step 3 position.

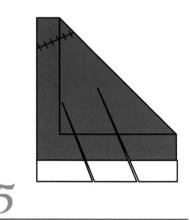

5

Cut off section as shown.

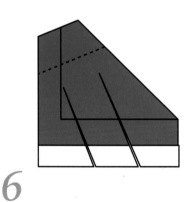

6

Valley folds both sides.

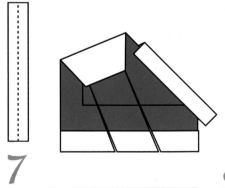

7

Trim strip length. Valley fold then glue. Squash fold.

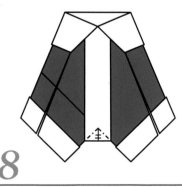

8

Cut and mountain folds.

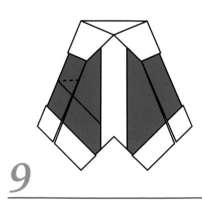

9

Valley fold arm.

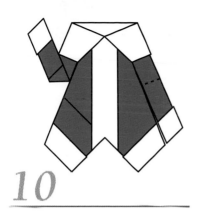

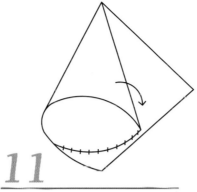

10

Valley fold other arm.

11

Roll a new sheet into cone. Glue and cut off excess.

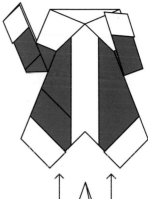

12

Insert cone into Santa's robe for better stability. Glue to hold.

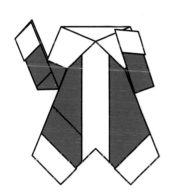

13

Completed part 3 (body) of Santa. (Liner hidden.)

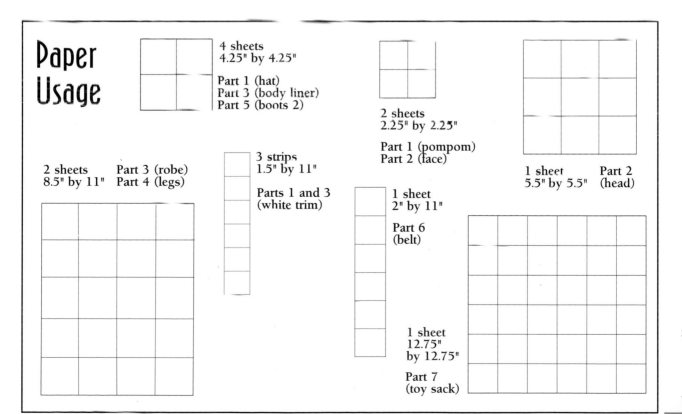

Paper Usage

4 sheets
4.25" by 4.25"

Part 1 (hat)
Part 3 (body liner)
Part 5 (boots 2)

2 sheets
2.25" by 2.25"

Part 1 (pompom)
Part 2 (face)

1 sheet
5.5" by 5.5"

Part 2 (head)

2 sheets   Part 3 (robe)
8.5" by 11"   Part 4 (legs)

3 strips
1.5" by 11"

Parts 1 and 3
(white trim)

1 sheet
2" by 11"

Part 6
(belt)

1 sheet
12.75"
by 12.75"

Part 7
(toy sack)

Santa Claus

73

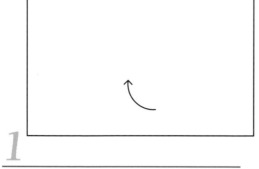

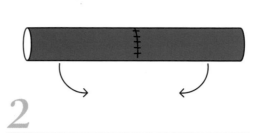

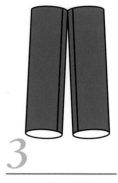

1 Roll rectangular sheet lengthwise into tube, and glue to hold.

2 Partially cut tube in center, then pull in direction of arrows.

3 Completed legs.

Part 5

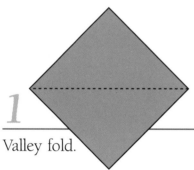

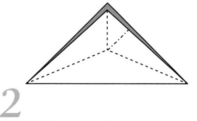

1 Valley fold.

2 Pinch top layer together, mountain fold as shown.

3 Mountain fold, then valley folds.

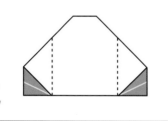

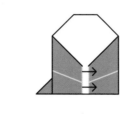

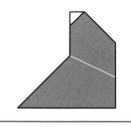

4 Valley folds.

5 Pull together as shown and glue to hold.

6 Completed part 5 (boot) of Santa. Now repeat (make 2).

Part 6

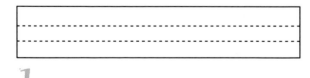

1 Strip of paper, valley fold in thirds.

2 Cut top layer as shown, then mountain fold flap to reverse side. Turn over.

3 Completed part 6 (belt) of Santa.

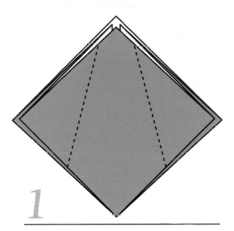

1
Start with step 6 of Base Fold III. Valley fold.

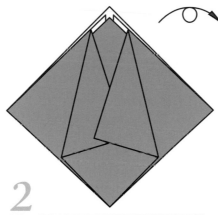

2
Apply glue, then turn over.

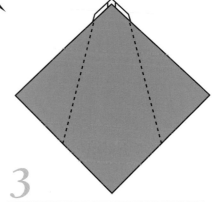

3
Valley folds and glue.

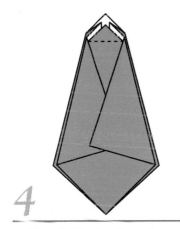

4
Valley folds both sides.

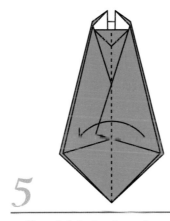

5
Valley folds both sides.

6
Valley folds both sides.

7
Push bottom upward and open top. (Open only one side when attaching to Santa.)

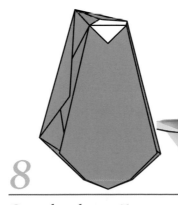

8
Completed part 7, Santa's toy sack.

Santa Claus

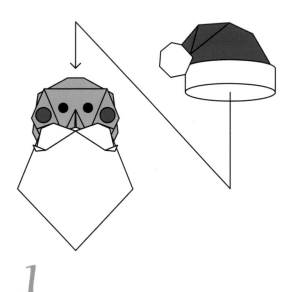

1

Attach hat to head.

2

Glue head part 2) onto body (part 3) and add belt (part 6).

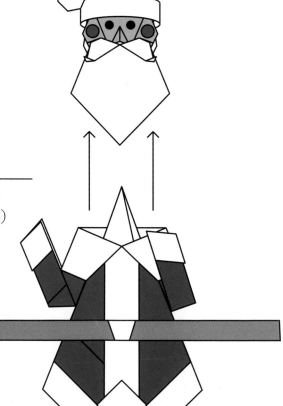

3

Glue sack (part 7) onto shoulder, if wanted. Attach boots (part 5) to legs (part 4) and legs to body, in standing or sitting position.

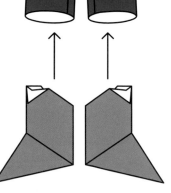

4

Completed Santa Claus standing…and sitting.

Reindeer

Part 1

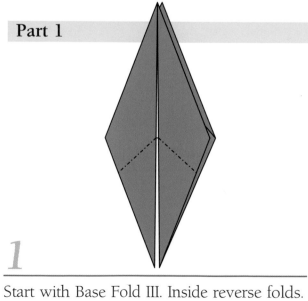

1

Start with Base Fold III. Inside reverse folds.

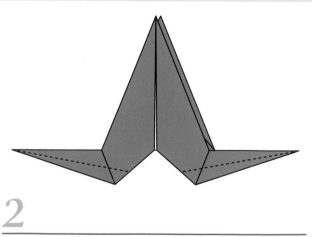

2

Valley folds both sides.

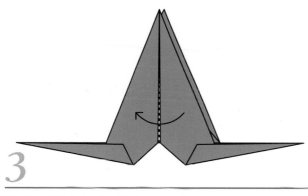

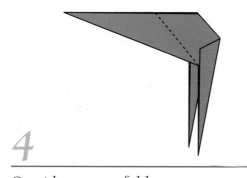

3

Valley fold in half. Rotate form.

4

Outside reverse fold.

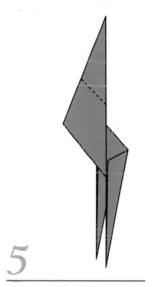

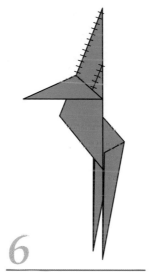

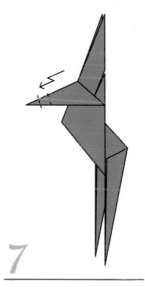

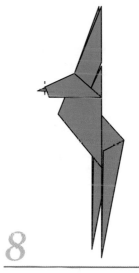

5

Outside reverse folds.

6

Make cuts as shown.

7

Pleat folds.

8

Outside reverse fold.

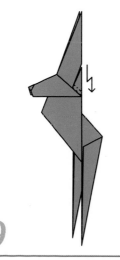

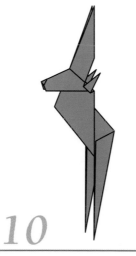

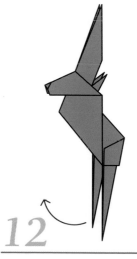

9

Pleat folds both sides.

10

Tuck ears in.

11

Pleat folds.

12

Pull and crimp fold.

13

Inside reverse folds.

14

Mountain folds both sides.

15

Cuts and valley folds.

16

Complete part 1 (front) of reindeer.

Part 2

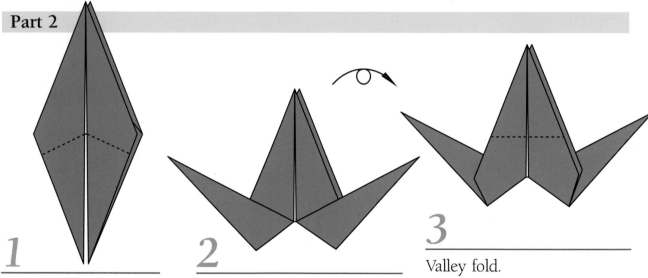

1

Start with Base Fold III. Valley folds.

2

Turn over to other side.

3

Valley fold.

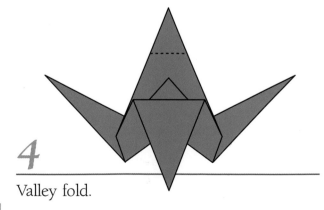

4

Valley fold.

5

Valley folds.

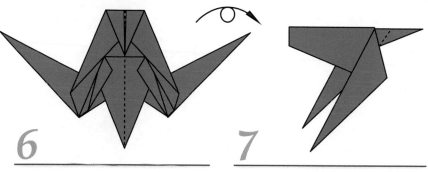

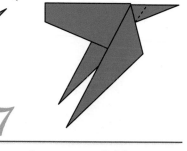

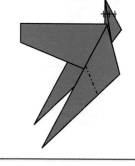

6

Fold in half, then rotate.

7

Outside reverse fold.

8

Inside reverse fold, both sides.

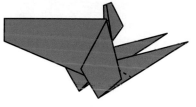

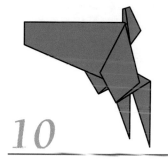

9

Inside reverse folds, both sides.

10

Completed part 2 (rear) of reindeer.

To Attach

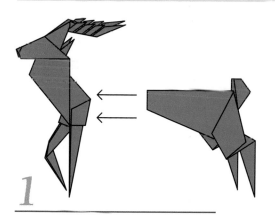

1

Join both parts together, and apply glue to hold.

2

Completed Reindeer.

Santa's Sleigh

Part 1

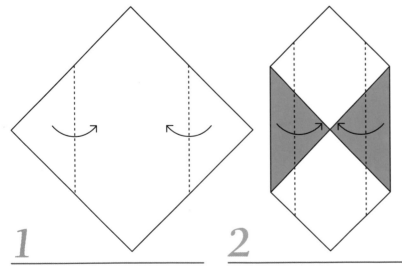

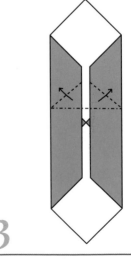

1

Valley folds to center.

2

Again, valley folds to center.

3

Valley/mountain folds to boxlike shape, glue to hold.

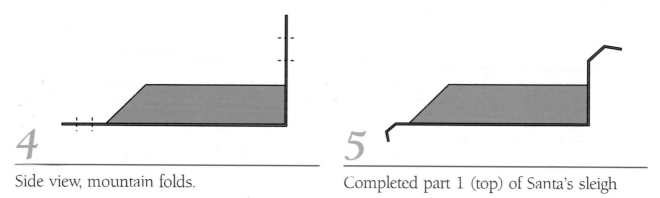

4

Side view, mountain folds.

5

Completed part 1 (top) of Santa's sleigh

Part 2

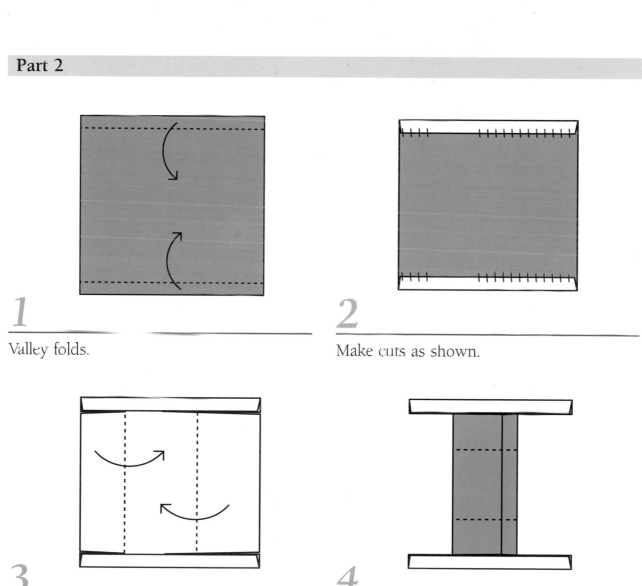

1

Valley folds.

2

Make cuts as shown.

3

Valley folds, right side then left.

4

Valley folds.

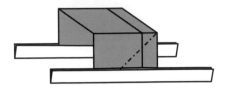

5

Mountain folds both sides.

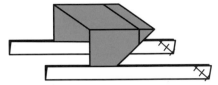

6

Make cuts as shown, and discard.

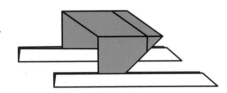

7

Completed part 2 (runners) of Santa's sleigh.

To Attach

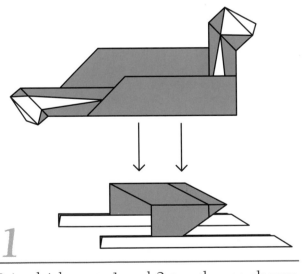

1

Join sleigh parts 1 and 2 together as shown and apply glue to hold.

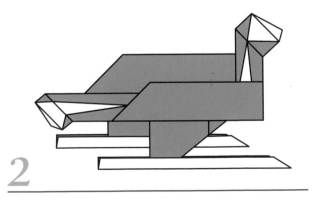

2

Completed Santa's Sleigh.

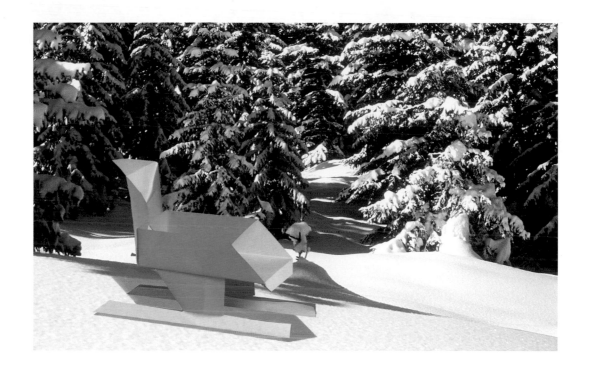

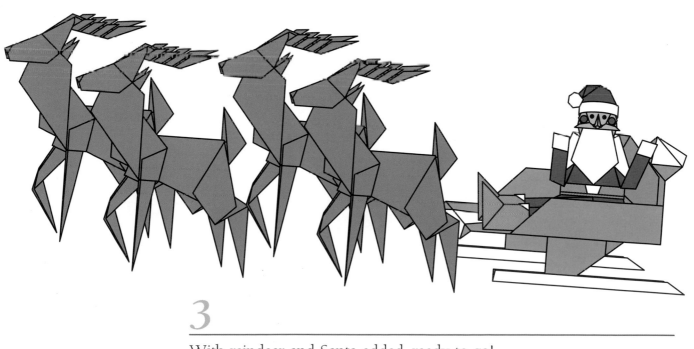

3

With reindeer and Santa added, ready to go!

Easter Bunny

Part 1

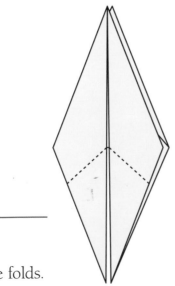

1

Start with
Base Fold III.
Inside reverse folds.

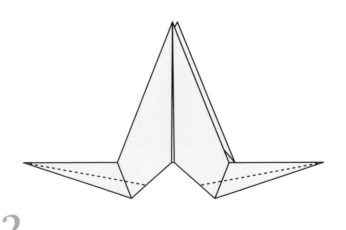

2

Valley folds both sides.

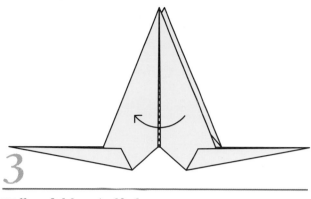

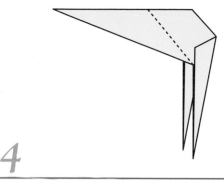

3

Valley fold in half, then rotate.

4

Outside reverse fold both layers together.

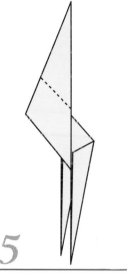

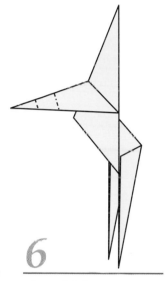

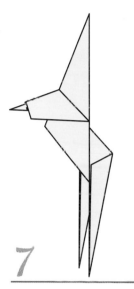

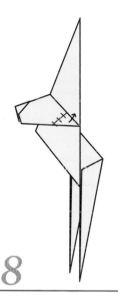

5

Outside reverse fold.

6

Pleat fold.

7

Outside reverse fold.

8

Cuts and valley open, both sides.

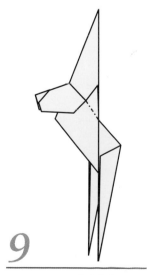

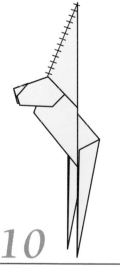

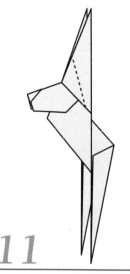

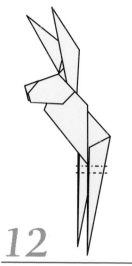

9

Mountain fold flaps.

10

Cut as shown.

11

Valley folds.

12

Pleat folds.

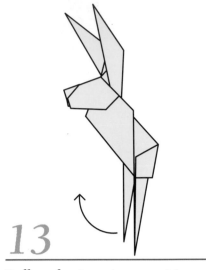

13

Pull and crimp into position.

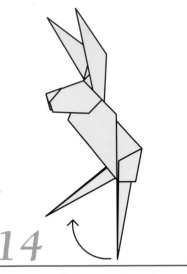

14

Again, pull forward and squash fold.

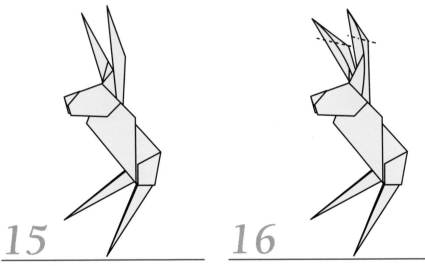

15

Pull open ears.

16

Valley folds.

17

Inside reverse fold.

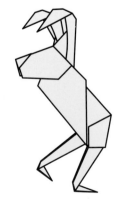

18

Completed part 1 (front) of Easter Bunny.

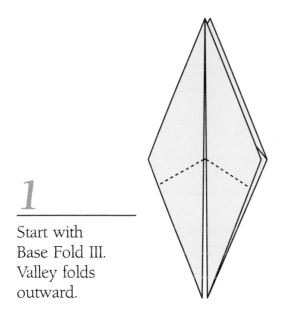

1

Start with
Base Fold III.
Valley folds
outward.

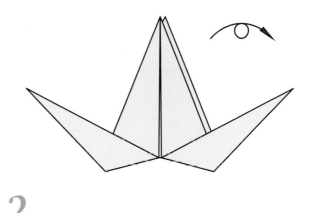

2

Turn over to other side.

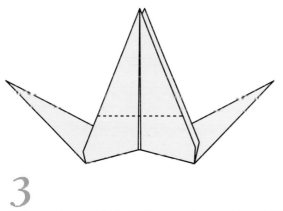

3

Valley fold.

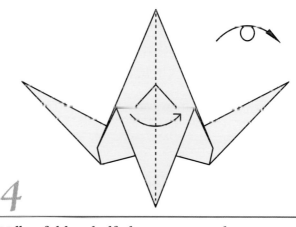

4

Valley fold in half, then rotate and turn over.

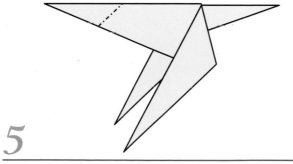

5

Inside reverse fold.

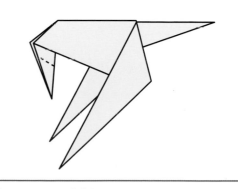

6

Outside reverse fold.

Easter Bunny

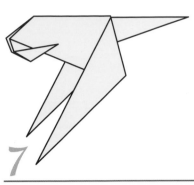

7

Tuck tip into center layers.

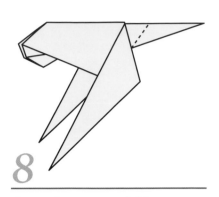

8

Outside reverse fold.

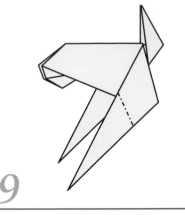

9

Inside reverse folds.

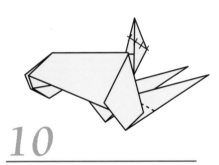

10

Inside reverse folds.

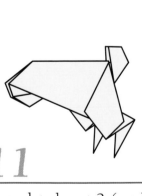

11

Completed part 2 (rear) of Easter Bunny.

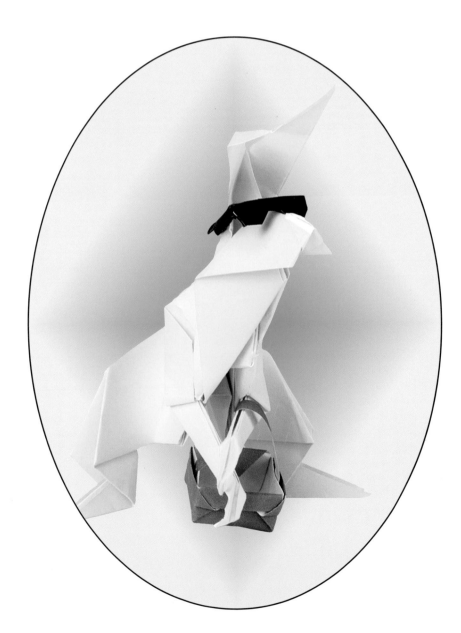

To Attach

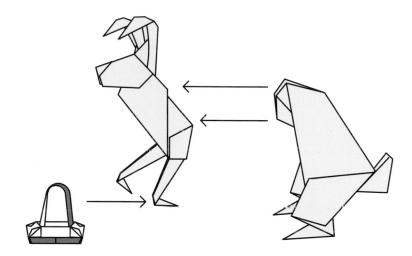

1

Join parts 1 and 2 together as shown, and apply glue to hold.

Provide bunny with basket (see next project).

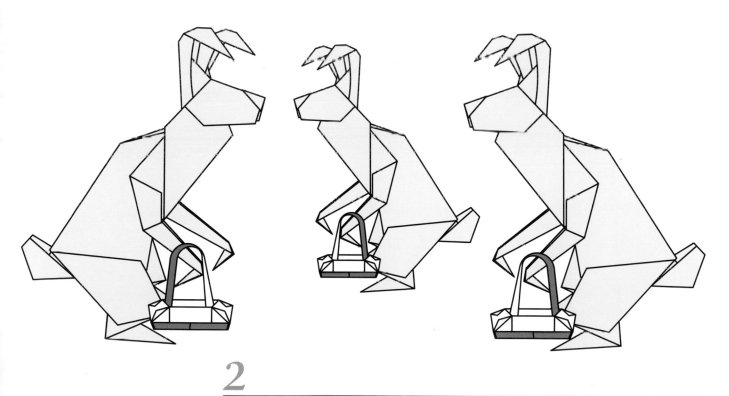

2

Completed Easter Bunny...and helpers.

Easter Basket

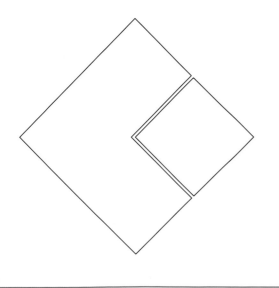

1

For small size, use ¼ of sheet.

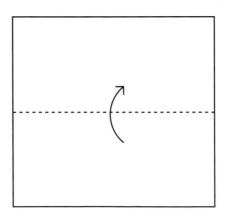

2

Valley fold.

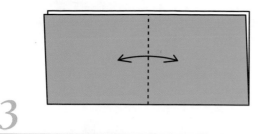

3

Valley fold, then unfold.

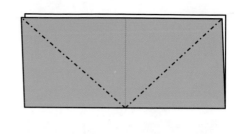

4

Inside reverse folds.

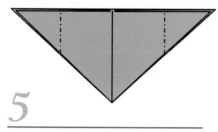

5

Inside reverse folds
all four corners.

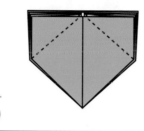

6

Valley fold both sides.

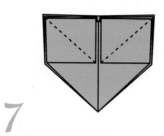

7

Valley folds.

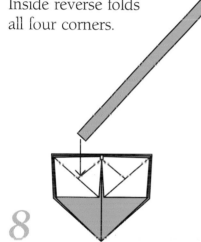

8

Add strip of paper.

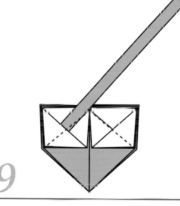

9

Valley folds.

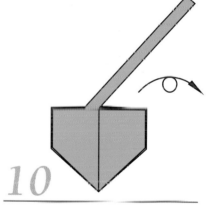

10

Turn over to other side.

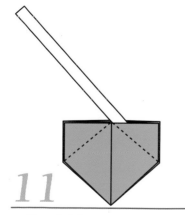

11

Valley folds.

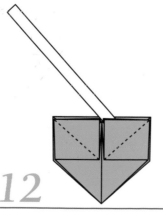

12

Valley folds.

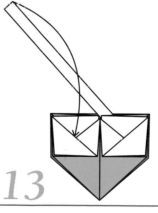

13

Insert strip as shown.

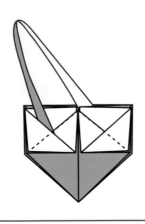

14

Valley folds.

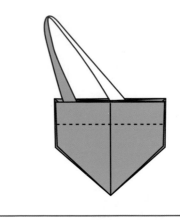

15

Valley folds both sides.

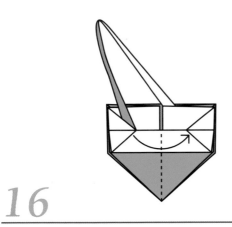

16

Valley folds.

17

Valley folds.

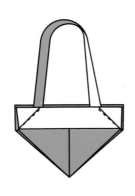

18

Valley folds.

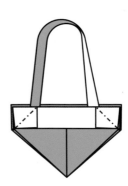

19

Mountain folds.

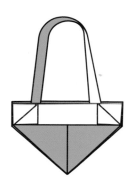

20

Repeat on all basket corners.

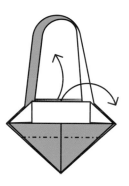

21

Pull to open out basket, mountain folding bottom to flatten.

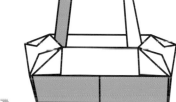

22

Completed Easter Basket. Larger baskets can be filled with eggs and other items as decoration.

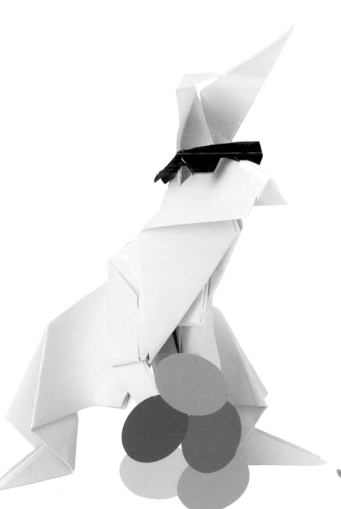

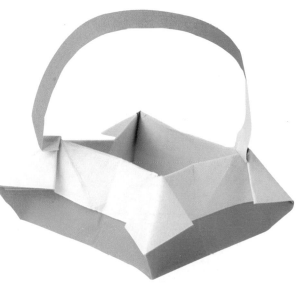

Index

angel, 48–53
cat's skull, 26–29
construction lines, 4
Easter basket, 92–95
Easter Bunny, 86–91
folds, base, 10–13
  I, 10
  II, 11
  III, 12–13
folds, basic, 6–9
  inside crimp fold, 9
  inside reverse fold, 7
  kite fold, 6
  mountain fold, 6
  outside crimp fold, 9
  outside reverse fold, 7
  pleat fold, 8
  pleat fold reverse, 8

squash fold I, 8
squash fold II, 9
valley fold, 6
gremlin mask, 44–47
Grim Reaper, 30–37
inside crimp fold, 9
inside reverse fold, 7
Jack-o'-Lantern, 14–17
kite fold, 6
Kris Kringle, 58–67
mountain fold, 6
outside crimp fold, 9
outside reverse fold, 7
paper usage
  angel, 51
  Grim Reaper, 31
  Kris Kringle, 65
  Santa Claus, 73

scarecrow, 21
witch, 42
paper, origami, 5
pleat fold reverse, 8
pleat fold, 8
reindeer, 78–81
Santa Claus, 68–77
Santa's sleigh, 82–85
Santa's toy sack, 75
scarecrow, 18–25
snowman, 54–57
squaring off paper, 17
squash fold I, 8
squash fold II, 9
symbols/lines, 5
technique, 4, 5
valley fold, 6
witch, 38–43